OCCASIONAL PAPER 268

Structural Reforms and Economic Performance in Advanced and Developing Countries

Jonathan D. Ostry, Alessandro Prati, and Antonio Spilimbergo

INTERNATIONAL MONETARY FUND
Washington DC
2009

© 2009 International Monetary Fund

Production: IMF Multimedia Services Division
Figures: Theodore F. Peters, Jr. and Tom Wood
Typesetting: Alicia Etchebarne-Bourdin

Cataloging-in-Publication Data

Ostry, Jonathan D., 1962–
  Structural reforms and economic performance in advanced and developing countries / Jonathan D. Ostry, Alessandro Prati, and Antonio Spilimbergo—Washington, D.C.: International Monetary Fund, 2009.

  p.; cm.—(Occasional paper (International Monetary Fund); no. 268).

  Incudes bibliographical references.
  ISBN 978-1-58906-818-6

  1. Structural adjustment (Economic policy)—Developed countries. 2. Structural adjustment (Economic policy)—Developing countries. I. Prati, Alessandro, 1961–. II. Spilimbergo, Antonio. III. International Monetary Fund. IV. Title. V. Series: Occasional Paper (International Monetary Fund); no. 268.

HD87.O88 2009

Please send orders to:
International Monetary Fund, Publication Services
700 19th Street, N.W., Washington, D.C. 20431, U.S.A.
Tel.: (202) 623-7430   Fax: (202) 623-7201
E-mail: publications@imf.org
Internet: www.imfbookstore.org

Contents

Preface		v
I	**Overview**	1
II	**Introduction**	2
III	**Structural Reforms: Measurement and Trends**	4
	Measuring Structural Reforms	4
	Trends in Structural Reform Since the 1970s	5
IV	**Determinants of Structural Reforms**	8
	Institutional Quality	8
	International Factors	8
	IMF-Supported Programs	10
	Economic Crises	10
V	**Structural Reforms and Economic Growth**	13
	Financial Sector Reforms	13
	Real Sector Reforms	25
VI	**Sequencing Real and Financial Sector Reforms**	33
VII	**Financial Sector Reforms and Resilience**	38
VIII	**Conclusions**	43
Appendix Data, Sources, and Methods		44
References		48

Boxes

3.1	Structural Reform Dataset	5
4.1	Democracy and Reforms	10
5.1	New-Schumpeterian Growth Specification	17
5.2	Determinants of Financial Development	20
7.1	Banking Sector Competition and Macroeconomic Stability	42

Figures

3.1	Economic Liberalization Indices	6
3.2	Economic Liberalization Indices by Income Group	7
4.1	Institutional Quality and Timing of Major Reforms	9
5.1	Financial Sector Reform and Growth	14

CONTENTS

5.2	Growth Breaks and Financial Sector Reforms	15
5.3	Financial Depth and Domestic Financial Sector Liberalization	19
5.4	Growth Breaks and Real Sector Reforms	26
6.1	Growth Breaks and Sequencing of Reforms	35
7.1	Financial Sector Reforms, Output Volatility, and Capital Account Crises	39
7.2	Terms of Trade Shocks and the Financial Sector	40

Tables

4.1	Determinants of Reforms	12
5.1	Growth Regression Results: Financial Sector Reforms (1)	16
5.2	Growth Regression Results: Financial Sector Reforms (2)	18
5.3	Effects of Financial Sector Reforms on Financial Depth	19
5.4	Foreign Direct Investment Inflows and Financial Sector Reforms	22
5.5	The Differential Effects of Financial Reforms in Manufacturing Industries	23
5.6	Financial Sector Reforms and Foreign Currency Bond Ratings	24
5.7	Growth Regression Results: Real Sector Reforms (1)	27
5.8	Growth Regression Results: Real Sector Reforms (2)	28
5.9	Trade Reforms and Export- and Import-to-GDP Share	29
5.10	The Differential Effects of Trade Reforms in Manufacturing Industries	30
5.11	Real Sector Reforms and Foreign Currency Bond Ratings	31
5.12	Effects of Trade Reforms on Financial Depth	32
5.13	Foreign Direct Investment Inflows and Real Sector Reforms	32
6.1	Sequencing of Structural Reforms	34
6.2	Growth Effects of Alternative Reform Sequencing Strategies	36
6.3	Cumulative Growth Effects of Alternative Reform Sequences: A Numerical Example	36
7.1	Financial Sector Reforms, Output Volatility, and Capital Account Crises	40
7.2	Financial Sector Reforms and Resilience to Terms of Trade Shocks	41
A1	List of Economies in the Sample	44
A2	Description of Reform Indices	45

The following conventions are used in this publication:

- In tables, a blank cell indicates "not applicable," ellipsis points (. . .) indicate "not available," and 0 or 0.0 indicates "zero" or "negligible." Minor discrepancies between sums of constituent figures and totals are due to rounding.

- An en dash (–) between years or months (for example, 2007–08 or January–June) indicates the years or months covered, including the beginning and ending years or months; a slash or virgule (/) between years or months (for example, 2007/08) indicates a fiscal or financial year, as does the abbreviation FY (for example, FY2008).

- "Billion" means a thousand million; "trillion" means a thousand billion.

- "Basis points" refer to hundredths of 1 percentage point (for example, 25 basis points are equivalent to ¼ of 1 percentage point).

As used in this publication, the term "country" does not in all cases refer to a territorial entity that is a state as understood by international law and practice. As used here, the term also covers some territorial entities that are not states but for which statistical data are maintained on a separate and independent basis.

Preface

This paper examines the impact on economic performance of structural policies—that is, policies that increase the role of market forces and competition in the economy, while maintaining appropriate regulatory frameworks. It examines the effects of structural reforms on two aspects of economic performance—medium-run growth and macroeconomic stability and resilience—from a global standpoint, and in so doing improves the analytical basis of IMF policy advice by drawing on the lessons from broad cross-country experience. Underpinning the results was a major data collection effort, involving the compilation of indicators of structural reform for a large sample of 91 developing and developed countries over the past three decades. The resulting dataset is unique in its country and time coverage. Compared to most previous efforts, it is also much broader in terms of the sectoral coverage of reforms—including indicators of liberalization in domestic product markets, international trade, several indicators of liberalization of the domestic financial sector, and measures of external capital account liberalization. The dataset's breadth along the sectoral dimension is essential to address issues of reform sequencing, an area that has generated much thought from a theoretical standpoint, but where systematic cross-country evidence—as opposed to smaller-scale case studies—is sorely lacking.

The paper was prepared under the direction of Jonathan D. Ostry (Deputy Director, Research Department) by a staff team led by Alessandro Prati (Chief, Macroeconomic Studies Division in the Research Department) and Antonio Spilimbergo, and comprising Lone Christiansen, Prachi Mishra, Chris Papageorgiou, Rodney Ramcharan, Martin Schindler, Nikola Spatafora, Stephen Tokarick, and Thierry Tressel. The paper has benefited from comments from a number of IMF colleagues. Special thanks are due to Manzoor Gill and Freddy Cama for outstanding research support, and to Tracey Lookadoo whose help ensured the timely preparation of the manuscript. Esha Ray of the External Relations Department edited the manuscript and coordinated its publication. The opinions expressed in this paper are those of the authors and do not necessarily represent the views of national authorities, the IMF, or IMF Executive Directors.

This paper is dedicated to the memory of Alessandro Prati.

1 Overview

Economic policy agendas in member countries—even as they have been dominated over the past year by the response to the global financial crisis—will, going forward, increasingly need to refocus on core issues related to strengthening medium-term economic performance, including both average growth and resilience to shocks. This paper examines the contribution of structural policies—that is, policies that increase the role of market forces and competition in the economy, while maintaining appropriate regulatory frameworks to deal with market failures—to economic performance. The results are based on a new dataset covering reforms of domestic product markets, international trade, the domestic financial sector, and the external capital account, in 91 developed and developing countries. The key results are:

- There has been a broad tendency to pursue structural reforms across all segments of the IMF's membership over the past three decades. Reforms have been driven by a number of factors, including the quality of broad political institutions in advanced economies early in the sample, and a catch-up effect spurring reform in developing countries subsequently, as sizable cross-country reform gaps—with respect to either reform "leaders" or reformist "neighbors"—emerged. There is also evidence that IMF-supported programs and, in the case of some sectors, economic crises have helped to catalyze structural reforms.

- Real and financial sector reforms have boosted per capita income growth in all segments of the Fund's membership, with domestic financial sector liberalization, trade liberalization, and farm sector liberalization exerting particularly large effects.

- Financial sector reforms have raised growth through a number of channels, including a reduction in domestic credit constraints and larger inflows of foreign direct investment (FDI). Structural reforms have exerted (statistically and economically) meaningful effects on allocative efficiency, as firms across different sectors react to the shifts in comparative advantage brought about by deregulation. The growth effects of financial and real sector reforms also reflect a more favorable assessment of the future profitability and solvency of domestic firms as embodied in their credit ratings.

- Growth effects differ significantly across alternative reform sequencing strategies. A trade-before-capital-account strategy achieves better outcomes than the reverse sequence, or even more than a "big bang" where reforms are pursued together. Liberalizing the domestic financial sector together with the external capital account is also growth-enhancing, provided the economy is relatively open to international trade. While the data do not speak loudly on the relative growth benefits of pursuing domestic financial reform versus external capital account liberalization early in the reform process, the stability benefits of early domestic financial sector liberalization dominate those of early capital account liberalization.

- The stability benefits flowing from domestic financial sector reform are also evident in the way in which economies respond to real and financial shocks, with relatively liberalized domestic financial sectors reducing the output costs from adverse terms of trade and interest rate shocks. A variety of mechanisms—especially improvements in credit availability—play a key role in enhancing the economy's resilience to shocks.

II Introduction

Even though economic policies in both developed and developing countries have been dominated for much of the past year by the response to the global financial crisis, going forward, countries will increasingly need to refocus on issues related to strengthening medium-term economic performance, including economic growth and resilience. The IMF has a key role to play, through its surveillance activities, in advising country authorities on these issues, including leveraging the lessons from cross-country experience for policy formulation at the national level, and drawing implications about the kind of policies that lead to more favorable "real-financial" linkages in response to country and global shocks. The IMF's role is tied to its responsibilities under Article IV of the Articles of Agreement to ensure that members' economic policies foster sound medium-term economic growth and stability.

The stability-cum-growth objective, while very broad, is linked to policies geared to strengthening market incentives and raising economic efficiency; boosting the sustainable rate of potential growth; and enhancing the economy's ability to absorb shocks. This, of course, is the traditional purview of structural policies, that is, policies that increase the role of market forces and competition in the economy, including by fostering both domestic and international trade and financial flows, while maintaining appropriate regulatory frameworks in the case of market failures or identified externalities. While progress has been made in understanding the role of such policies, empirical evidence based on a consistent global dataset is lacking, with previous studies focused mainly either on the experience of industrial countries or of the transition economies. The paucity of comparable data on indicators of structural reform across the full gamut of different income groups and regions has undoubtedly been a factor behind the lack of global reach of past empirical studies.

This paper examines the effects of structural reforms on two aspects of economic performance—medium-run growth and macroeconomic stability and resilience—from a global standpoint, and in so doing improves the analytical basis of IMF policy advice by drawing on the lessons from broad cross-country experience. Underpinning the results is a significant data collection effort, involving the compilation of indicators of structural reform for a large sample of 91 developing and developed countries over the past three decades. Not only is the resulting dataset unique in its country and time coverage, it also is much broader in terms of the sectoral coverage of reforms—including indicators of liberalization in domestic product markets, international trade, several indicators of liberalization of the domestic financial sector, and measures of the external capital account liberalization. The dataset's breadth along the sectoral dimension is essential to address issues of reform sequencing, an area that has generated much thought from a theoretical standpoint, but where systematic cross-country evidence—as opposed to smaller-scale case studies—is sorely lacking.

The analysis in the paper yields a number of significant results:

- There has been a broad tendency to pursue structural reforms across all segments of the IMF's membership over the past three decades. Low- and middle-income countries have on average reached the degree of liberalization achieved by the industrial countries in the early 1990s in the areas of product market and domestic financial sector liberalization, with larger, but shrinking, reform gaps in trade and external capital account liberalization.

- Reforms across the IMF's membership appear to have been driven by a number of factors, including the quality of broad political institutions in advanced economies early in the sample, and a significant catch-up effect spurring reform in developing countries subsequently, as sizable cross-country reform gaps—with respect to either reform "leaders" or reformist "neighbors"—emerged. There is also evidence that IMF-supported programs and, for some sectors, economic crises have helped to catalyze structural reforms.

- Real and financial sector reforms have exerted an economically significant impact on per capita income growth in all segments of the IMF's membership, with domestic financial sector liberalization, trade liberalization, and liberalization of the agricultural sector exerting particularly favorable effects. A number of channels are in evidence, including a reduction in credit constraints to, and borrowing costs for, capital accumulation, and larger inflows of FDI that seem to result from external capital account liberalization. There is also evidence that structural reforms help to raise allocative efficiency, as firms across different sectors react to the shifts in comparative advantage brought about by deregulation. Firms that are highly dependent on imported intermediate inputs in production, for example, see large growth benefits from trade liberalization, while firms with a high dependence on external finance for their investments see particular growth benefits from financial sector liberalization. The impact of financial and real sector reform on economic growth also seems to reflect a more favorable assessment of the future profitability and solvency of domestic firms as embodied in their credit ratings.

- Growth effects differ significantly across alternative structural reform sequencing strategies. There is strong evidence supporting the view that economies that liberalize trade before liberalizing the external capital account grow more rapidly than those that follow the reverse sequence. There is also evidence that a parallel pursuit of both domestic financial sector reform and external capital account liberalization—provided that the trade regime is relatively open—is a growth-friendly reform strategy. While the data do not speak loudly on the relative growth benefits of pursuing domestic financial sector reform versus external capital account liberalization early in the reform process, the stability benefits—in terms of both macroeconomic volatility and crisis propensity—are found to be more favorable when the domestic financial sector is liberalized ahead of the external capital account.

- The stability benefits flowing from domestic financial sector reform are also evident in the way in which economies respond to various real and financial shocks, with resilience—the bounce-back of the economy following a shock—enhanced in economies with relatively liberalized domestic financial sectors. Financial reforms tend to reduce the output costs from adverse terms of trade and foreign interest rate shocks, with a variety of mechanisms—especially improvements in credit availability—playing a key role. The greater resilience to real shocks in economies with more liberalized financial sectors is evidence of how such reforms can strengthen economy-wide real-financial linkages.

The remainder of the paper is organized as follows. Section III presents the main features of the dataset and key trends in structural reform over the past three decades. Section IV examines a range of factors that may serve to spur, or retard, the process of structural reform. The subsequent sections present empirical evidence on the impact of reforms, including their effects on economic growth (Section V), related sequencing issues (Section VI), and macroeconomic volatility and resilience (Section VII). Section VIII concludes.

III Structural Reforms: Measurement and Trends

Structural reforms are a more elusive concept to measure than, say, the tenor of standard macroeconomic policies, where gauges—interest rates, liquidity measures, or the budgetary balance—are typically readily available for most countries. In the realm of structural policies, by contrast, researchers generally need to peruse legal statutes and rule books and devise classification criteria to create indicators that measure reform in different sectors of the economy, and that can serve as inputs for empirical analysis.

Structural reforms are usually held to include policy measures that reduce or remove impediments to the efficient allocation of resources. In many cases, the efficient allocation may correspond to "laissez-faire" or the "free-market" outcome and, as such, structural reforms would imply reduced government intervention, including the removal of state-imposed price controls, the abolition of state monopolies, and fewer restrictions on trade and domestic or international financial transactions. But structural reforms may also encompass measures to address market failures not due to government intervention, including natural monopolies, dominant market positions, or distortions in the financial sector arising, for example, from asymmetric information and moral hazard. Following this broader view, the indices of structural reform described below include measures of "effective regulation" to address potential market failures in product and financial markets. To take an example, countries with well-supervised banking systems will score highly on the banking liberalization index described below, even though banking regulation and supervision is a departure from laissez-faire.

Measuring Structural Reforms

This paper draws on an extensive dataset, compiled by the IMF's Research Department, which brings together information on a variety of structural reforms in different sectors over roughly the past 30 years, and that covers a cross-section of both industrial and developing countries. The new dataset thus has significant advantages over existing data sources that cover a narrower set of reforms and countries, and is likely to be useful not only for the analysis carried out below, but also more broadly for the IMF's surveillance activities (see Box 3.1 and Appendix Tables A1 and A2 for further details).

Reform indicators cover both the realm of the "financial sector" and the "real sector," though, as will be evident in subsequent sections, financial sector reforms have important effects on real sector outcomes, and vice versa, given the significance of macro-financial linkages inherent in economic performance. Financial sector reform indicators include reforms pertaining to domestic financial markets, including banking and securities markets, as well as the external capital account, while real sector structural reform indicators include measures of product market and trade reforms.[1]

All indicators are scaled to vary between zero and unity, with higher values representing greater liberalization. Differences in the values of each index across countries and over time provide information on the variation in the absolute degree of economic reform within each sector. However, indices are not strictly comparable across sectors, so a higher value of, say, the trade reform index than the banking reform index does not imply that an economy is "more liberal" with respect to international trade than domestic finance.

Turning first to financial reforms, the *domestic financial sector liberalization* indicator includes measures of securities markets and banking sector reform. The *securities markets* subindex assesses the quality of the market framework, including the existence of an independent regulator and the extent of legal restrictions on the development of domestic bond and equity markets. The *banking* subindex captures reductions or removal of interest rate controls (floors or ceilings), credit controls (directed credit and subsidized lending), competition restrictions (limits on branches and entry barriers in the banking market, including licensing requirements or limits on foreign banks), and public ownership of banks. As foreshadowed above, the banking index also captures a measure of the quality

---

[1]Data on labor market and fiscal reforms are being gathered, but cross-country coverage, especially for emerging market and developing countries, remains insufficient for inclusion in the analysis.

Trends in Structural Reform Since the 1970s

> **Box 3.1. Structural Reform Dataset**
>
> The main features of the dataset used in this paper are described below, with further technical details provided in Appendix Tables A1 and A2.
>
> **Domestic financial sector reforms.** This indicator extends the country and time coverage of the domestic financial sector components in Abiad and Mody (2005), and adds a component covering credit controls (see Abiad, Detragiache, and Tressel, 2008). The index thus covers six broad areas: interest rate controls, entry barriers, privatization, supervision and regulation, securities markets, and credit controls. Other relevant work includes Williamson and Mahar (1998), who record financial reforms in 34 countries over 1973–96 along the same dimensions as Abiad and Mody (2005); Bekaert, Harvey, and Lundblad (2005), who date equity market liberalizations in 95 countries during 1980–95; and the European Bank for Reconstruction and Development's (EBRD) dataset of transition indicators for 29 nonindustrialized countries over 1989–2007 (published annually in the EBRD's *Transition Report*), which includes variables that measure banking and securities market reform gaps with industrialized market economies.
>
> **Capital account reforms.** The data collected cover controls on external borrowing and lending as well as other restrictions on financial transactions between residents and nonresidents, including approval requirements for foreign direct investment. The sources are Abiad, Detragiache, and Tressel (2008) and Quinn (1997), extended to include additional countries and years. Other relevant work includes Schindler (2009), which constructs a disaggregated capital controls index for 91 countries over 1995–2005 and reviews other related indices.
>
> **Product market reforms.** The product market reform index covers the agricultural sector and the telecommunications and electricity sectors, and comprises simplified versions of existing indices produced by the Organization for Economic Cooperation and Development (OECD), extended to include non-OECD countries. Relevant data by the OECD include an index of regulatory reform in the telecommunications, electricity, gas, post, rail, air passenger transport, and road freight sectors (Conway and Nicoletti, 2006), and the OECD's producer and consumer support estimates of agricultural policies during 1986–2006 (published as a complement to the OECD report *Agricultural Policies in OECD Countries: Monitoring and Evaluation 2007*). Other relevant work includes the World Bank's Doing Business database (http://www.doingbusiness.org/), which provides measures of business regulations for a large number of countries during 2004–07; and the EBRD's transition indicators database, containing variables pertaining to telecommunications and electricity liberalization in transition countries.
>
> **Trade reforms.** There are two indices: the first is an extension of the database on average tariff rates in IMF (2004) to include non-OECD countries and a broader time coverage; the second is based on Quinn (1997), and captures the degree to which proceeds from international trade in goods and services are free from restrictions as defined under Article VIII, extended to include additional countries and years. Other relevant work includes Sachs and Warner (1995), who provide a binary measure of trade liberalization based on a mix of regulatory and outcomes-based information; and the EBRD's transition indicators database, which contains variables pertaining to liberalization of trade and the foreign exchange system in transition economies.

of banking supervision and regulation, including the power and independence of bank supervisors, the adoption of Basel capital standards, and the presence of a framework for bank inspections.

Regarding the extent of *external capital account liberalization*, the data collected cover a broad set of restrictions including, for example, controls on external borrowing between residents and nonresidents, as well as approval requirements for FDI.

Turning to structural reforms in the real sector, the first indicator measures reductions in public intervention in the *agricultural sector*, including removal of export marketing boards and reductions in the incidence of administered prices. The second indicator covers the degree of liberalization in the *telecommunications and electricity markets*, including the extent of competition in the provision of these services and the presence of an independent regulator. The third index captures liberalization of *international trade* along two dimensions: *tariff liberalization*, which measures average tariff rates; and a broader indicator of *current account liberalization*, which captures surrender requirements for export proceeds, and other items under Article VIII of the Fund's Articles of Agreement.

Trends in Structural Reform Since the 1970s

Figures 3.1 and 3.2 portray the broad global trend toward greater structural reform and liberalization over the past three decades across different segments of the IMF's membership. Some key points follow from the figures:

- *Domestic financial sector reforms and the opening of the capital account accelerated sharply in the early 1990s*, reflecting, inter alia, the expansion of the European Union (which involved harmonization of financial legislation and regulation across member countries), the accession of a number of emerging market countries to

III STRUCTURAL REFORMS: MEASUREMENT AND TRENDS

the Organization for Economic Cooperation and Development, and the economic transition of Central and Eastern Europe.

- *Both measures of trade liberalization follow a gradual upward trend with a noticeable pickup since the late 1980s*, reflecting the pursuit by developing countries of greater trade liberalization in the aftermath of the debt crisis, and more generally the demise of import substitution policies pursued earlier. The global context of several rounds of multilateral and regional trade negotiations also contributed.

- *Liberalization of the agricultural sector gathered speed during the 1990s*, with the adoption of more market-friendly policies in the developing world. This partly reflected an emphasis on such policies in World Bank structural adjustment lending, as well as falling agricultural prices, which made marketing boards less sustainable.

- *In the telecommunications and electricity sectors, deregulation began in earnest in the second half of the 1990s*, reflecting to a large degree innovations in communications technology—such as cellular phones and the diffusion of the Internet—that exposed public telecommunications monopolies to competition.

- Regarding trends in structural reform across different income groups, *advanced economies began implementing reforms relatively early*, and these "first movers" have also progressed the furthest with structural reform. This being said, *emerging market and developing countries are catching up with advanced economies in the level of liberalization achieved*, with a substantial narrowing of the reform gap in evidence for all sectors since the mid-1980s. To take an example, the average level of domestic financial sector reform in low- and middle-income countries is now comparable to that of high-income countries in the early 1990s.

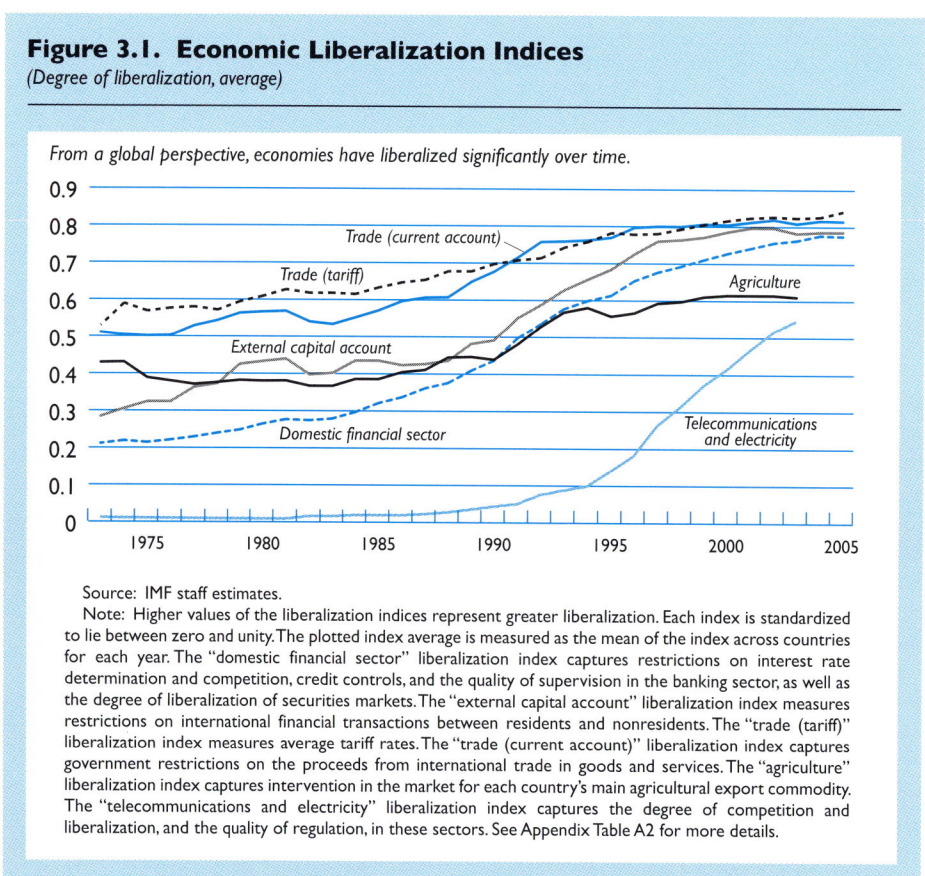

Figure 3.1. Economic Liberalization Indices
(Degree of liberalization, average)

From a global perspective, economies have liberalized significantly over time.

Source: IMF staff estimates.
Note: Higher values of the liberalization indices represent greater liberalization. Each index is standardized to lie between zero and unity. The plotted index average is measured as the mean of the index across countries for each year. The "domestic financial sector" liberalization index captures restrictions on interest rate determination and competition, credit controls, and the quality of supervision in the banking sector, as well as the degree of liberalization of securities markets. The "external capital account" liberalization index measures restrictions on international financial transactions between residents and nonresidents. The "trade (tariff)" liberalization index measures average tariff rates. The "trade (current account)" liberalization index captures government restrictions on the proceeds from international trade in goods and services. The "agriculture" liberalization index captures intervention in the market for each country's main agricultural export commodity. The "telecommunications and electricity" liberalization index captures the degree of competition and liberalization, and the quality of regulation, in these sectors. See Appendix Table A2 for more details.

Figure 3.2. Economic Liberalization Indices by Income Group
(Degree of liberalization)

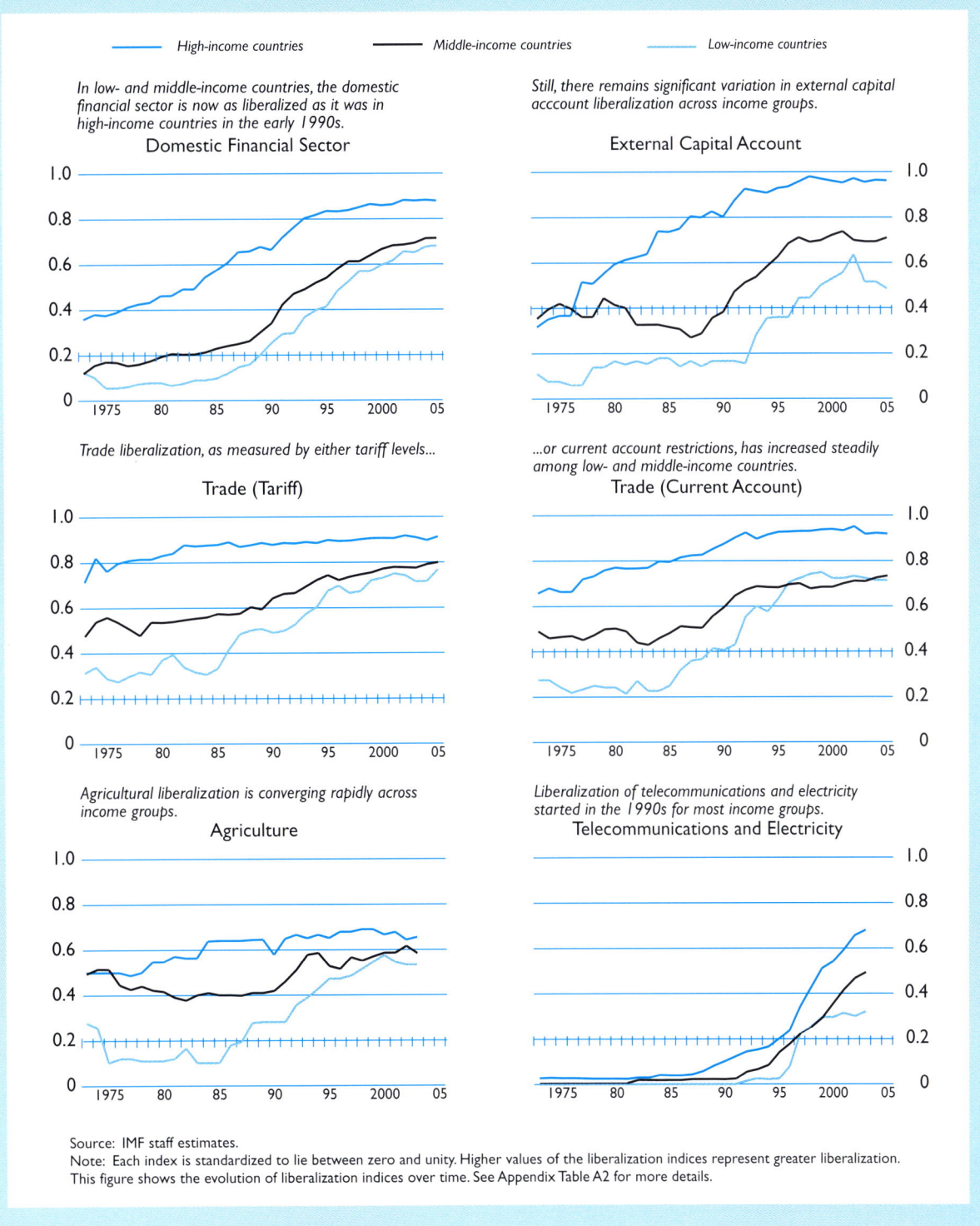

Source: IMF staff estimates.
Note: Each index is standardized to lie between zero and unity. Higher values of the liberalization indices represent greater liberalization. This figure shows the evolution of liberalization indices over time. See Appendix Table A2 for more details.

IV Determinants of Structural Reforms

The political economy literature has tended to emphasize that special interests, motivated by a desire to protect rents, may act to block the introduction of reforms that are beneficial for society at large. Previous work, including for example IMF (2004) and Høj and others (2006), has highlighted a number of factors that can affect the balance of power between pro- and anti-reform groups. Such factors include the quality of broad political institutions, which may favor an early adoption of reforms; international factors, including the size of "reform gaps" vis-à-vis either countries at the "frontier" of the reform process or geographical neighbors that may spur reform through "peer pressure" channels; the presence of an IMF-supported program, which may serve to underpin the reform process; and the occurrence of economic crisis, which is often argued to be a catalyst of reform. This section presents evidence on the role of these factors in both developed and developing countries.

Institutional Quality

Institutions define the broad rules of the game within which economic agents influence the outcome of the reform process. How does the quality of broad political institutions affect progress with implementing structural reforms? Figure 4.1 sheds light on the issue by portraying the relationship between the timing of major reforms and the level of the institutional quality index. It shows that, on average for most sectors, countries with stronger institutions (proxied by the strength of property rights and the rule of law as measured by Kaufmann, Kraay, and Zoido-Lobatón, 2002) have introduced major reforms earlier, that is, there is a negative relationship between the year of major liberalizations and institutional quality. The results appear to be strongest for trade liberalization (as measured by the tariff-based indicator), and for the domestic financial sector and external capital account liberalization indicators.

In addition to broad institutional quality, as captured by property rights and rule of the law, there may be specific political institutions that foster or hinder economic reforms. Box 4.1, which is based on Giuliano, Mishra, and Spilimbergo (2008) analyzes the role of one such specific institution: the quality of democracy in a country. Democracy is measured using the standard, well-established measure of democracy from the Polity IV database. Empirical evidence strongly suggests that raising the quality of democratic institutions has a positive and statistically significant impact on economic reforms.

As foreshadowed earlier, a range of other factors may also play a role in determining the pace of structural reform. A regression framework is useful to disentangle the various effects, recognizing of course that a number of possible determinants—including, for example, the level of per capita income or educational attainment—are, like the quality of broad institutions, highly persistent, and therefore likely to be captured by the "fixed" or country effects in the regression framework.[2]

International Factors

Table 4.1 considers first the effect of the "reform gap," defined as the (lagged) difference between the level of liberalization in a particular country and the reform level achieved in a country near the reform "frontier" (proxied here by the United States). The results suggest that a larger reform gap is associated with faster reforms in all sectors, as indicated by the positive and statistically significant coefficient in the first row of Table 4.1. Beyond liberalization gaps with respect to reform *leaders*, the proximity of reformist *neighbors* may also provide a stimulus for liberalization. Table 4.1 indicates that such "neighborhood effects" operate unevenly across sectors, with statistically significant effects in evidence only in the cases of the domestic financial sector and the telecommunications and electricity sectors (second row of Table 4.1).

---

[2]In practice, given the inclusion of fixed effects, the results in Table 4.1 focus on variables with a sufficient variability over time. The model without fixed effects (not reported) shows a statistically significant impact on the pace of structural reform of a number of the persistent factors mentioned in the text, including a positive effect of institutional quality on trade, domestic financial sector, and external capital account reforms, consistent with the evidence in Figure 4.1.

Figure 4.1. Institutional Quality and Timing of Major Reforms

Source: IMF staff estimates based on Kaufmann, Kraay, and Zoido-Lobatón (2002).
Note: The year of liberalization portrayed on the x-axis is the year of major reform—as measured by a one standard deviation or higher increase in the liberalization index over the preceding three years. The y-axis measures institutional quality, which is taken from Kaufmann, Kraay, and Zoido-Lobatón (2002), and captures the protection afforded to property rights as well as the strength of the rule of law, circa mid-1990s. This figure shows that major reforms occur earlier in countries where the quality of broad political institutions is higher, that is, the relationship between institutional quality and the year of liberalization is negative.

IV DETERMINANTS OF STRUCTURAL REFORMS

Box 4.1. Democracy and Reforms

Empirical evidence on the relationship between democracy and the adoption of economic reforms is scarce and limited to particular types of reforms and a small sample of countries. This box is based on Giuliano, Mishra, and Spilimbergo (2008), and studies the impact of democracy on the adoption of economic reforms using the new dataset on structural reforms.

Numerous theoretical arguments and historical examples suggest that political freedom can either hinder or facilitate economic reforms. A fully democratic regime can fall prey to interest groups, which put their goals before the general well being of citizens. In particular, interest groups can block reforms if there is uncertainty about the distribution of the benefits (Fernandez and Rodrik, 1991). On the other hand, in a newly independent country, a "benevolent dictator" can shelter the institutions, avoid that the state becomes captive of any specific interest group, and allow the state to perform its function in an efficient way.[1] Take the historical examples of Chile, or Korea. In both cases, important economic reforms were undertaken under dictatorial regimes. The majority of the contemporary industrialized countries were not democracies when they took off (see Schwarz, 1992). In most cases, East Asian economies did not develop under fully democratic regimes. In addition to pressure from interest groups, democracy can lead to excessive private and public consumption and lack of sufficient investment (Huntington, 1968). Wages are typically higher under democracy (Rodrik, 1999). In contrast, dictatorial regimes can rely on financial repression to increase the domestic saving rate. Several countries with repressive political and highly regulated financial systems, including the Soviet Union and many East Asian economies, were

Democracy and Reforms

Dependent variable: Change in liberalization index (t)	
Democracy ($t-1$)	0.025***
	(0.005)
International factors	
Reform gap ($t-1$)	0.081***
	(0.006)
Reform in neighbors ($t-1$)	0.176***
	(0.036)
IMF-supported program ($t-1$)	0.009***
	(0.002)
Economic crisis ($t-1$)	0.001
	(0.004)
Observations	9,440
Number of countries	102

Sources: IMF staff estimates based on IMF, *International Financial Statistics*, and the Polity IV database.

Notes: The table shows regressions of the annual change in each liberalization index on democraccy (lagged). Democracy is measured using the Polity IV database. The polity index is normalized so that 1 indicates the most democratic country and 0 the least democratic regime. See notes to Table 4.1 for detailed description of the controls. Regressions include country and reform fixed effects. Robust standard errors are provided in parentheses. ***, **, and * denote statistical significance at the 1, 5, and 10 percent level, respectively.

able to increase savings and achieve sustained high economic growth rates.

The alternative view that democracy often accompanies economic reforms is also based on strong theoretical arguments. In general, dictators cannot credibly take commitments so any reform that involves problems of time-consistency cannot be undertaken (McGuire and Olson,

---

[1]Along these lines, Haggard (1990) argues that "Institutions can overcome collective-action dilemmas by restraining the self-interested behavior of groups through sanctions: collective action problems can be resolved by command."

IMF-Supported Programs

Previous studies (e.g., Ghosh and others, 2005) have suggested that structural conditionality in IMF-supported programs may play a role in spurring structural reform. The regression framework in Table 4.1 investigates this issue by including an indicator variable for the presence of an IMF-supported program. The results suggest that programs do seem to play a catalytic role in accelerating reforms across most of the sectors. The finding that IMF-supported programs accelerate the pace of liberalization of the external capital account, however, should be interpreted alongside the evidence presented in IEO (2005), which stresses the role of domestic ownership of capital account liberalization policies rather than IMF conditionality per se in the pursuit of such policies.

Economic Crises

While there is considerable anecdotal evidence to suggest a catalytic role of economic/financial crises in driving the reform process, whether this constitutes an empirical regularity is an issue that needs to be decided by recourse to the data. What, then, is the

1996). Autocratic rulers tend to be predatory so disrupting economic activity and making any reform effort meaningless; autocratic regimes also have an interest in postponing reforms and maintaining rent-generating activities for a restricted number of supporting groups. On the other hand, democratic rulers should be more sensitive to the interests of the general public, and so more willing to implement reforms that destroy monopolies in favor of the general interests.

The sharp contrast between these opposing views implies that the question is primarily an empirical one. While there is a vast amount of theoretical and empirical literature that considers the determinants of economic reforms in general, there is little empirical evidence on the relationship between democracy and reforms. The existing papers focus on reforms in particular sectors, such as international trade and finance, or specific countries over a short period of time, such as the post-communist economies. Giuliano, Mishra, and Spilimbergo (2008), instead, use the newly constructed large dataset on reform indicators to analyze the impact of democracy on economic reforms. Democracy is measured using the standard, well-established measure of democracy from the Polity IV database.[2] The index is normalized so that 1 indicates the most democratic country and 0 the least democratic regime. Economic reform is defined as a positive annual change in the liberalization index. Reform indicators in different sectors are pooled in order to study the effect of democracy on the general ability of a country to undertake structural reforms in any sector. In addition, pooling of reforms allows one to obtain more precise estimates by increasing the number of observations substantially.[3]

The table shows the results from a panel regression framework, where reforms are regressed on lagged level of democracy and several controls. The regressions include country fixed effects to control for institutional differences across countries that are time-invariant. In addition, reform fixed effects control for differences across sectors. The coefficient on the lagged level of democracy is significant at the 1 percent level. The estimated coefficient suggests that a one standard deviation increase in the quality of democratic institutions explains about 9 percent of the variability in reforms.[4]

The theoretical predictions about the feedback effect from economic reforms to democratization are ambiguous as well. For example, economic liberalizations could be associated with a higher quality of democratic institutions if they increase the power of the middle class (Rajan and Zingales, 2003). On the other hand, liberalization could lower democracy through increases in income inequality and the associated political strife and violence (Quinn, 1997; and Dixon and Boswell, 1996). Overall, the empirical findings suggest that while democracy promotes reform, there is no evidence that economic reforms promote the process of political liberalization.

---

[2]The measure captures the quality of democratic institutions, on the basis of freedom of active and passive participation in elections, checks and balances on the executive, freedom of political association, and respect of other basic political rights.

[3]Giuliano, Mishra, and Spilimbergo (2008) show that with the exception of the telecommunications and electricity sector, democracy promotes reforms in all sectors.

[4]The estimated coefficient on democracy is unchanged if one includes additional determinants of reforms in the regressions, for instance, alternative indicators of crisis, human capital and bureaucratic quality, public expenditures, indicators for ideology of government (left, right, or center), form of government (presidential or parliamentary) and additional political variables such as number of executive constraints, the presence of legislative or executive elections, the number of years left in the current term for the executive, and the presence of an absolute majority in the legislature by the party of the executive. In addition, the results are robust to using an instrumental variables strategy, where democracy in neighboring countries is used as an instrument.

---

evidence on the role of economic crises in the reform process? The results in Table 4.1 indicate that the effect of crises on the pace of reform is mixed, with the data suggesting that crises play little systematic role in a preponderance of the sectors. Crises do appear to spur domestic financial sector reform, but actually seem to delay opening to international trade—possibly reflecting the need to secure additional sources of fiscal revenue in crises periods, including by recourse to higher tariffs.

Overall, the results in Table 4.1 and Figure 4.1 suggest that, while institutional quality served to underpin structural reforms among the industrial countries in the early years of the sample, the emergence of sizable cross-country reform gaps contributed to an acceleration of reform among the developing countries in the sample, especially since the early 1990s. Peer pressure effects associated with neighboring reformers supported the reform process in some areas, including domestic financial sector liberalization. Among the other factors driving reform, the presence of an IMF-supported program appears to have played a role in accelerating reforms in a number of sectors, while the occurrence of crises has tended to spur domestic financial sector reform and retard trade reform.

IV DETERMINANTS OF STRUCTURAL REFORMS

Table 4.1. Determinants of Reforms

Dependent Variable: Change in Liberalization Index (t)	Domestic Financial Sector Liberalization (1)	External Capital Account Liberalization (2)	Trade Liberalization (Tariff) (3)	Trade Liberalization (Current Account) (4)	Agricultural Liberalization (5)	Telecommunications and Electricity Liberalization (6)
International factors						
Reform gap (t–1)	0.041*** (0.010)	0.155*** (0.014)	0.195*** (0.016)	0.074*** (0.012)	0.105*** (0.013)	0.055*** (0.016)
Reform in neighbors (t–1)	0.179*** (0.061)	0.143 (0.094)	0.108 (0.067)	0.114 (0.092)	0.063 (0.059)	0.327*** (0.074)
IMF-supported program (t–1)	0.049*** (0.015)	0.091** (0.039)	0.092* (0.052)	0.060* (0.031)	0.002 (0.03)	0.082*** (0.027)
Economic crisis (t–1)	0.024*** (0.005)	–0.02 (0.013)	–0.022*** (0.007)	0.004 (0.009)	0.008 (0.009)	–0.005 (0.007)
Observations	1,565	1,565	2,100	1,130	1,676	1,678
Number of countries	64	64	102	38	75	76

Sources: IMF staff estimates based on IMF, *International Financial Statistics*.

Notes: The table shows regressions of the annual change in each liberalization index on a number of covariates. These include international factors (a measure of reform gaps vis-à-vis the United States and a measure of the level of liberalization in neighboring countries where the neighborhood is based on geographical distance); the presence of an IMF-supported program; and a measure of economic crisis defined as episodes of high inflation. The measure of reform gaps is defined as the difference between the reform level achieved in a country near the reform "frontier" (proxied by the United States) and the level of liberalization in a particular country. The measure of reform in neighbors is calculated for each country as the weighted average of all other countries' liberalization indices, with the weights proportional to the inverse of their distance to the country under consideration. The variable "IMF-supported program" takes a value of unity in country-years when such a program is in place. The variable "economic crisis" is an indicator variable that takes a value of unity in country-years when inflation is above 40 percent; the results are robust to alternative measures of crisis used in the literature, including sharp drops in output, large terms of trade shocks, and sizable real devaluations. Robust standard errors are provided in parentheses. ***, **, and * denote statistical significance at the 1, 5, and 10 percent level, respectively.

Robustness: To address possible endogeneity, the indicator variable for an IMF-supported program is instrumented using a measure of political proximity to, and trade intensity with, the United States and Europe, as in Barro and Lee (2005). All specifications are estimated by panel instrumental variable regressions with country fixed effects, using annual data over 1973–2004. The country fixed effects capture the impact on the reform process of all time-invariant country-specific factors, including persistent differences in income per capita across countries. The results are robust to using five-year changes in each liberalization index as the dependent variable (instead of the annual changes reported in the table). The estimates are broadly similar when additional international factors are included. For example, adding indicator variables for World Trade Organization and Organization for Economic Cooperation and Development memberships—which affect positively trade and financial sector reforms—leaves key results unchanged.

V Structural Reforms and Economic Growth

There is a broad consensus in the literature that structural reforms, and in particular measures aimed at promoting domestic financial development and trade liberalization, can be important components of a strategy to invigorate economic growth.[3] Structural reforms may serve to boost aggregate income by promoting both faster capital accumulation and a more efficient allocation of resources. These benefits are typically spread over time, but forward-looking financial markets may anticipate the future benefits of reform, which would then be reflected in such forward-looking variables as credit ratings and borrowing costs.

While existing empirical studies generally support this line of reasoning, in a number of respects they fall short of providing a firm basis for policy. First, a global perspective based on a consistent data source spanning different segments of the IMF's membership has thus far been lacking. Second, existing studies have not tackled empirically key issues related to the interactions among reforms and sequencing, which have a critical bearing on growth.

Third, previous studies have paid insufficient attention to the *channels* through which reforms affect growth. Evidence on such channels is needed to underpin confidence in the robustness of the observed empirical linkages. The remainder of this section considers, in turn, the impact of financial and real sector reforms on growth, focusing both on the aggregate effects and some key channels through which they may operate. The analysis focuses on the ceteris paribus effects of one reform at a time, with sequencing issues taken up in Section VI.

Financial Sector Reforms

Financial sector reforms may raise growth by helping to mobilize savings and thereby expanding the availability of credit, as well as by improving the allocation of capital in the economy.[4] Prima facie, the data—across both developed and developing countries—do suggest that more financially liberalized economies enjoy faster growth, on average, over the sample (Figure 5.1). An economy with a domestic financial sector reform index above the median grows on average 1.3 percentage points faster than an economy below the median, with a higher score in each of the component (banking and securities market) reform subindices contributing to higher growth. The differential growth performance in favor of countries with relatively open, versus relatively closed, external capital accounts is positive but small (last two columns of Figure 5.1).

---

[3]McKinnon (1973), Krueger (1997), and Henry (2007) are among the seminal studies supporting this view. The literature is not, of course, all to one side on the role of reforms in the growth process. Easterly (2005), for instance, focuses on the association between a larger set of economic policies (price distortions, financial development, trade openness, and macroeconomic policies) and growth. Easterly's baseline growth regression suggests that improvement in the considered policy dimensions leads to a substantial increase in income per capita growth. Nevertheless, once the sample is restricted to exclude large outliers, any association between policy variables and growth disappears. Hausmann, Pritchett, and Rodrik (2005) discuss how policies aimed at promoting economic growth can be highly context-specific.

Recent literature also investigates whether institutions are more relevant than policies to explain country-wide differences in economic performance. Easterly and Levine (2003) ask whether policies such as openness to international trade, inflation, and impediments to international transactions matter to explain current differences in income levels. The evidence they provide suggests that macroeconomic policies are not very relevant to explaining the current level of economic development once the impact of the institutions on economic development is taken into account. They argue that bad policies might be "symptoms" of deeper institutional failures. Acemoglu and others (2003) reach a similar conclusion. Once the historically determined component of institutions is controlled for, economic policies play a small role in explaining economic volatility, crises, and growth. Distortionary policies are likely to be mirroring the existence of weak institutions.

[4]A large literature suggests that a well-developed financial sector promotes economic growth (Levine, 2005). However, relatively few studies try to assess the impact of financial sector reforms on economic growth. Bekaert, Harvey, and Lundblad's (2005) main measure of financial liberalization is a dummy variable equal to one for the years in which foreign investors may own equities in a particular market. Equity market liberalization increases annual real per capita GDP growth by almost 1 percent. Quinn and Toyoda (2008) provide detailed de jure measures of capital account and financial current account openness and document that capital account liberalization is positively associated with growth. Finally, recent empirical work provides evidence that structural reforms improve economic performance in advanced economies. Nicoletti and Scarpetta (2003), using an original dataset on product market regulation in 18 OECD countries, show that product market reforms that promote private corporate governance, competition, and privatization raise productivity growth.

V STRUCTURAL REFORMS AND ECONOMIC GROWTH

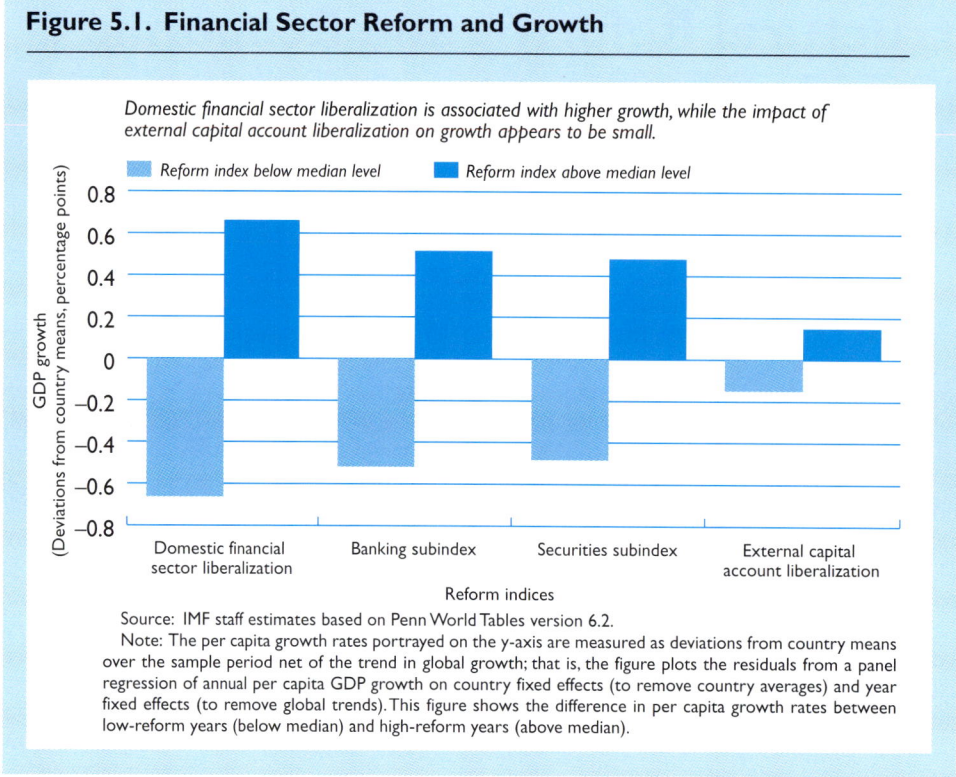

Figure 5.1. Financial Sector Reform and Growth

What lies behind the finding that economies with more liberalized domestic financial sectors enjoy faster growth? From an empirical standpoint, an answer to this question should take into account the very different features of the growth experience of developed and developing countries. While output paths in the former tend to resemble reasonably steady "hills," in developing countries output paths are often characterized by "mountains, cliffs, and plains" (Pritchett, 2000), which suggests that focusing on determinants of a country's *average* growth rate, as portrayed in Figure 5.1, may miss important elements of the transmission channels from liberalization to growth. From this standpoint, across a broad sample of developing and advanced economies, an approach based on linking structural reform to growth accelerations and decelerations ("mountains and cliffs"), rather than average growth, may be more revealing. Such an approach is portrayed in Figure 5.2, which plots the behavior of financial reforms in the period leading up to, and following, growth upbreaks and downbreaks.[5]

Two patterns emerge from Figure 5.2. First, both domestic financial/banking sector liberalization and external capital account liberalization increase in the run-up to growth accelerations. Second, the data suggest that growth downbreaks are associated with a high initial degree of external capital account liberalization; this result, however, needs to be interpreted with caution because, as discussed in the next subsection, external capital account liberalization appears to be detrimental for growth only if such liberalization precedes the opening of the trade account. The data do not suggest a strong effect of trends in domestic financial sector liberalization ahead of growth downbreaks.

Econometric evidence presented in Table 5.1 corroborates the finding of a favorable impact of financial reforms on growth accelerations. Controlling for a set of standard growth determinants, including lagged income per capita, educational attainment, a terms of trade index, and a measure of political institutions (democracy), an increase in the (lagged value) of each of the four main financial sector reform indicators has a positive, and statistically significant, effect on growth.[6] There are, however, impor-

---

[5]See the Appendix, as well as Berg, Ostry, and Zettelmeyer (2008) and Antoshin, Berg, and Souto (2008), for a deeper discussion of the statistical procedures used to identify upbreaks and downbreaks.

[6]The presence of a convergence term (lagged income per capita) in the regressions implies that a change in the level of reforms has a transitional effect on growth and a permanent effect on income. During the transition to the new post-reform steady state, growth rates will be higher than before, but will eventually return to their steady-state level (see, relatedly, Henry, 2007). This is in line with the graphical event study presented in Figure 5.2, which links reform to growth accelerations and decelerations. In practice, transitions across steady states last for many years, resulting in persistent increases in growth rates during the transition.

Figure 5.2. Growth Breaks and Financial Sector Reforms

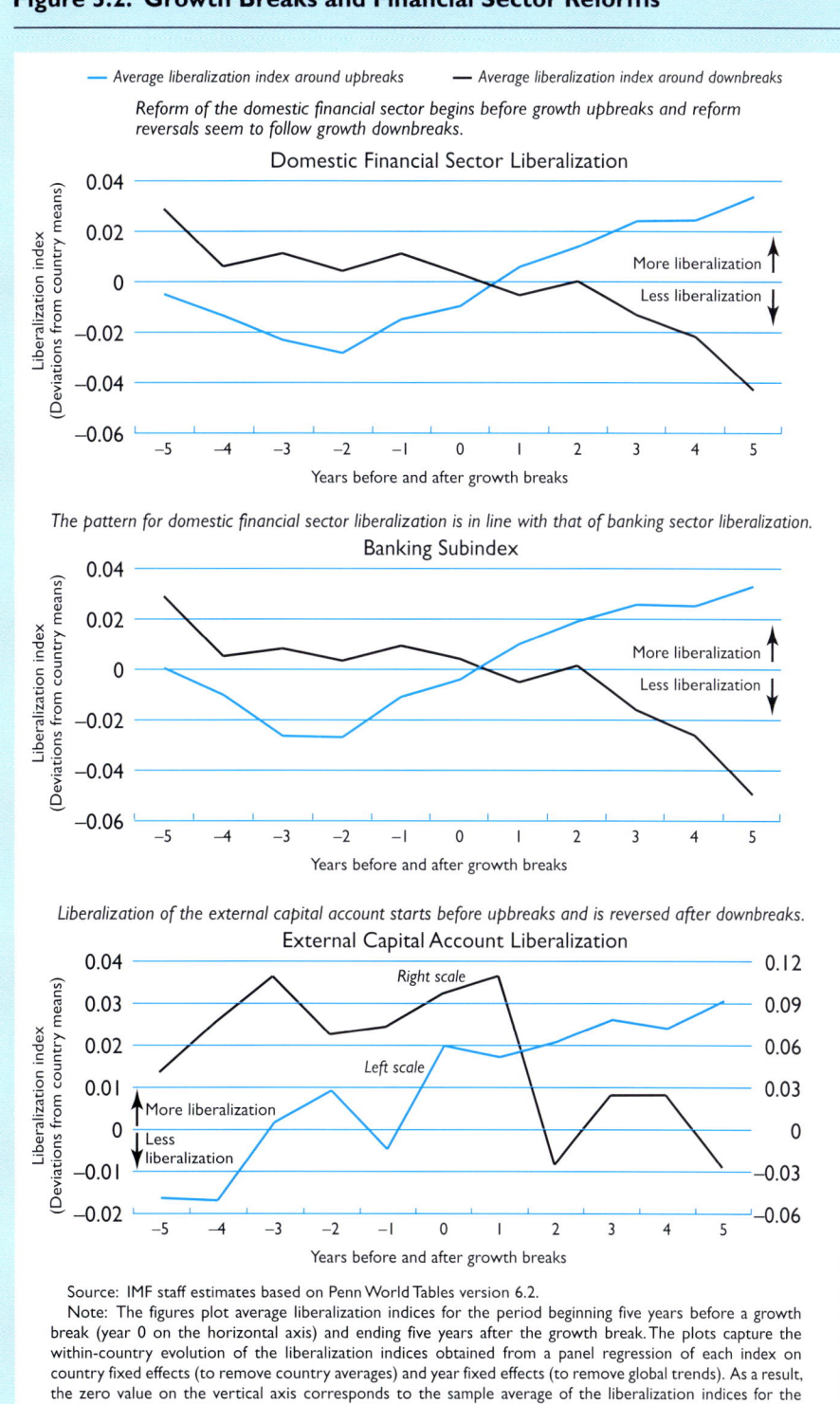

Source: IMF staff estimates based on Penn World Tables version 6.2.
Note: The figures plot average liberalization indices for the period beginning five years before a growth break (year 0 on the horizontal axis) and ending five years after the growth break. The plots capture the within-country evolution of the liberalization indices obtained from a panel regression of each index on country fixed effects (to remove country averages) and year fixed effects (to remove global trends). As a result, the zero value on the vertical axis corresponds to the sample average of the liberalization indices for the countries considered. The number of countries used to compute each average varies across indices in line with data availability.

V STRUCTURAL REFORMS AND ECONOMIC GROWTH

Table 5.1. Growth Regression Results: Financial Sector Reforms (1)

Dependent Variable: logGDP(t) − logGDP(t−1)	Domestic Financial Sector Liberalization (1)	Banking Subindex (2)	Securities Subindex (3)	External Capital Account Liberalization (4)
Entire sample				
Liberalization index (t−1)	0.060**	0.046***	0.035***	0.015***
	(0.012)	(0.011)	(0.007)	(0.005)
Long-run income effect: 25–75 percentile improvement	0.507***	0.364***	0.354***	0.154***
	(0.102)	(0.088)	(0.066)	(0.057)
Observations	2,114	2,114	2,114	2,114
Number of countries	88	88	88	88
Adjusted R-squared	0.13	0.13	0.13	0.12
Low- and middle-income group				
Liberalization index (t−1)	0.084***	0.066***	0.039***	0.018**
	(0.019)	(0.017)	(0.039)	(0.008)
Long-run income effect: 25–75 percentile improvement	0.557***	0.394***	0.171***	0.160***
	(0.130)	(0.105)	(0.046)	(0.071)
Observations	1,398	1,398	1,398	1,398
Number of countries	68	68	68	68
Adjusted R-squared	0.13	0.12	0.12	0.12

Sources: IMF staff estimates based on IMF, *International Financial Statistics*; Penn World Tables version 6.2; and World Bank, *World Development Indicators*.

Notes: The table shows regressions of annual growth in real GDP per capita on financial sector liberalization indicators. The regressions are estimated for the entire country sample and for the group of low- and middle-income countries (see Appendix Table A1). Each regression includes as controls the lagged level of real GDP per capita, an indicator variable for democratic regimes, the level of terms of trade, and the level of tertiary school enrollment. The long-run income effect captures the estimated change in the steady-state level of GDP per capita resulting from an improvement in the liberalization index from the 25th to the 75th percentile. All specifications were estimated by panel OLS with country and year fixed effects, using annual data over 1960–2005. Robust standard errors are in parentheses. The standard errors on the long-run effects are calculated with the delta method. ***, **, and * denote statistical significance at the 1, 5, and 10 percent level, respectively.

Robustness: To address possible endogeneity, all specifications were also estimated by panel 2SLS with country fixed effects and five-year lags of the liberalization index as instrument. The results are robust to this alternative specification. Most results hold also in regressions estimated on five-year nonoverlapping intervals with growth rates over a five-year period regressed on five-year lags of each liberalization index.

tant differences in the magnitude of the effects of each reform. Specifically, domestic financial sector reforms have a long-run impact on income per capita that is three to four times larger than that of external capital account liberalization. For example, an increase in the indices from the 25th to the 75th percentile of the distribution is associated with a rise in long-run per capita income of about 50 percent in the case of domestic financial sector reform compared to 15 percent for external capital account liberalization.[7] While liberalizations of such a magnitude are large, they have occurred in the sample, including, for example, during New Zealand's domestic financial sector reforms over 1983–86 and Chile's external capital account liberalization over 1997–2000. Finally, the second panel in Table 5.1 investigates whether there are significant differences in the impact of financial sector reforms across income groups. While the general tenor of the full-sample results holds across different income groups, the impact of banking sector reform on growth is much larger for the developing country group, possibly reflecting the greater importance of bank intermediation at lower income levels.

The regression results presented in Table 5.1 derive from the standard neoclassical growth theory and are well suited to evaluating the impact of reforms on the equilibrium level of income. However, for economies that are still far from the long-term equilibrium growth rate, the most relevant question is what factors explain the speed of convergence. In order to analyze this, the growth equation is now estimated on the full sample (as in Table 5.1), but each liberalization index is allowed to enter the specification both directly and interacted with the country's "income gap," that is, the ratio of its GDP to output in the world's richest economies (proxied by GDP in the United States). If a given interaction term is negative and statistically significant, then this implies

---

[7]About two-thirds of these effects occur within a two-decade horizon of the policy shock, while the impact (one-year) effects are about 5 percent of the long-run impact.

Box 5.1. New-Schumpeterian Growth Specification

An alternative to the neoclassical specification considered in Table 5.1 is the neo-Schumpeterian specification presented in Tables 5.2 and 5.8. This specification derives from Schumpeterian growth theory, which is based on the process of "creative destruction." Creative destruction, as discussed in the writings of Joseph Schumpeter (1928 and 1942), refers to the endogenous introduction of new products and processes, which inevitably eliminates some of the existing products and processes.

Schumpeterian growth theory has been revived and formally modeled by Aghion and Howitt (1992). A key implication of neo-Schumpeterian theory is that economic development can be evaluated by the distance of a country's per capita GDP from that prevailing in frontier countries. The most relevant question in neo-Schumpeterian growth literature is therefore how fast low-income countries can close the gap with the frontier (usually proxied by per capita GDP in the United States). Recent empirical research using the Schumpeterian specification has examined what drives the speed of income convergence among countries (see, e.g., Aghion and Howitt, 2005), stressing that some factors, such as high-quality institutions or high education levels, can speed up convergence.

As argued in Acemoglu, Aghion, and Zilibotti (2006) and van Elkan (1996), when a country is far from the world technology frontier, the most relevant source of growth is the adoption of already well-established technologies. The closer a country gets to the technological frontier, the more innovation matters for economic growth. In other words, the closer a country is to the world technological frontier, the higher is the relative importance of innovation versus imitation to sustain productivity growth. Consequently, the set of possible policies aimed at sustaining growth, what the authors define as "appropriate institutions," can vary for countries at different stages of economic development. Building on these theoretical insights, Aghion and Howitt (2005) analyze in depth the case of education. The authors argue that primary and secondary education matters more for a country's ability to imitate the frontier technology, while tertiary education has a larger impact on a country's possibility of innovating. As a country catches up to the technology frontier, tertiary education becomes more relevant to growth than primary/secondary education.[1] Vandenbussche, Aghion, and Meghir (2006) provide evidence for a panel of 19 OECD countries for the period 1960-2000 consistent with the idea that higher education matters more as a country catches up to the technological frontier.

The neo-Schumpeterian approach applied to the case of structural reform policies calls for an econometric specification such as that in Table 5.2. There are two main differences between this specification and the neoclassical specification in Table 5.1. First, convergence is now captured by an "income-gap" term that is measured by the ratio of per capita GDP in country j to per capita GDP in the United States (the country with the largest per capita GDP in our sample). Second, in addition to the reform variable, an interaction term between reform and "income-gap" is included to capture the potential effect of reforms in closing the gap relative to the level of output in the United States.

---

[1]Aghion and Howitt (2005) combine insights from Nelson and Phelps (1966) and Acemoglu, Aghion, and Zilibotti (2006). Nelson and Phelps model an economy where the productivity growth can be expressed according to the equation: $A = f(h)(\bar{A} - A)$, where h is the current stock of human capital in a country, and $\bar{A}$ is the frontier technology growing over time at some exogenous rate. A higher stock of human capital fosters growth by facilitating catching up to the technological frontier. In Aghion and Howitt (2005), analogously to Acemoglu, Aghion, and Zilibotti (2006), productivity growth can be generated either by imitating the frontier technology or by innovating on past technologies. The relative importance of innovation increases as a country gets closer to the technological frontier. Moreover, higher education investment should produce a bigger effect on a country's ability to make leading-edge innovation, while primary and secondary education should exert a larger impact on a country's ability to implement frontier technology.

---

that the growth returns from reforming that sector will be larger the further a country is from the world output frontier; in particular, the impact on growth will be relatively larger for low- and middle-income countries. Box 5.1 discusses in more detail the motivation for this alternative growth specification.

Table 5.2 shows that liberalizing the domestic financial sector, and more specifically the banking sector, not only has a larger direct effect on growth than opening the capital account, but also speeds up the convergence of a country's output level to that in frontier countries while an open capital account does not.

What are the key channels through which domestic and external financial liberalization contribute to an acceleration in growth? A well-established empirical result is that financial depth is strongly correlated with growth (see, e.g., Levine, 1997 and 2005). One expected channel is suggested by the positive association between domestic financial sector liberalization and financial depth, as portrayed in Figure 5.3. Hence, financial liberalization may lead to an acceleration in growth by removing constraints on the supply of capital and improving access to credit for businesses.

Empirical analysis suggests that financial reforms boost financial development, but only in environments in which individuals are well protected from the risks of expropriation. Indeed, regression analysis (Table 5.3) corroborates the favorable impact of banking reforms on the credit-to-GDP ratio. However, the effect is sustained in the medium term only in countries with adequate

V STRUCTURAL REFORMS AND ECONOMIC GROWTH

Table 5.2. Growth Regression Results: Financial Sector Reforms (2)

Dependent Variable: logGDP(t) − logGDP(t−1)	Domestic Financial Sector Liberalization (1)	Banking Subindex (2)	Securities Subindex (3)	External Capital Account Liberalization (4)
Entire sample				
Liberalization index (t−1)	0.083***	0.073***	0.034***	0.017**
	(0.0158)	(0.0150)	(0.0098)	(0.0085)
Liberalization index* (GDPj/GDPus)(t−1)	−0.059***	−0.064***	−0.009	−0.017
	(0.0193)	(0.0184)	(0.0156)	(0.0136)
Observations	2,114	2,114	2,114	2,114
Number of countries	88	88	88	88
Adjusted R-squared	0.12	0.12	0.11	0.10

Sources: IMF staff estimates based on IMF, *International Financial Statistics*; Penn World Tables version 6.2; and World Bank, *World Development Indicators*.

Notes: The table shows regressions of annual growth in real GDP per capita on real sector liberalization indicators. The regressions are estimated for the entire country sample (see Appendix Table A1). Each regression includes as controls the lagged ratio of the level of real GDP per capita in country j to the level of real GDP in the United States, an indicator variable for democratic regimes, the level of terms of trade, and the level of tertiary school enrollment. All specifications were estimated by panel OLS with country and year fixed effects, using annual data over 1960–2005. Robust standard errors are in parentheses. ***, **, and * denote statistical significance at the 1, 5, and 10 percent level, respectively.

Robustness: To address possible endogeneity, all specifications were also estimated by panel 2SLS with country fixed effects and five-year lags of the liberalization index as instrument. The results are robust to this alternative specification. Most results hold also in regressions estimated on five-year nonoverlapping intervals with growth rates over a five-year period regressed on five-year lags of each liberalization index.

checks and balances on political power (see Box 5.2). Moreover, not all dimensions of financial liberalization serve to boost credit growth: the removal of entry barriers and of restrictions on the allocation of credit have the most significant effect on financial deepening in developing countries, while improvements in supervisory and regulatory practices tend to reduce the credit-to-GDP ratio at impact (Table 5.3). The empirical analysis also confirms that good macroeconomic policies have a direct favorable effect on financial development.[8]

The finding that strong property rights may be a necessary condition for the banking system's functioning to improve after financial liberalization is consistent with Acemoglu and Johnson (2005), who find that more stringent constraints on the executive have a significant positive effect on growth, investment, and financial development.[9] They interpret their result as evidence that protection against expropriation by the state or by powerful elites helps develop financial systems.

Other researchers have found that, in addition to property rights protection, the cross-section of financial sector development is also explained by institutional country characteristics such as legal origin (La Porta and others, 1998), contracting rights institutions (Djankov, MacLiesh, and Shleifer, 2007), and political stability (Roe and Siegel, 2008). Macroeconomic factors (Boyd, Levine, and Smith, 2001; and Hauner, 2009) and the ownership of banks (La Porta, Lopez-de-Silanes, and Shleifer, 2002; and Detragiache, Tressel, and Gupta, 2008) are also determinants of financial development. Braun and Raddatz (2008), Baltagi, Demetriades, and Law (2007), and Hauner and Prati (2008) explore political economy theories of financial development by testing the hypothesis of Rajan and Zingales (2003) that financial development tends to occur when economies are opened up to foreign competition, so that the rents of incumbents who prevent broadening access to credit are eroded.

Turning to the role of external capital account liberalization, econometric results highlight a positive relationship between opening to external capital flows and the credit-to-GDP ratio (Table 5.3). In addition, fewer restrictions on capital movements seem to be associated with significantly higher FDI inflows (Table 5.4) which, as argued in Dell'Ariccia and others (2008), tend to be growth enhancing.[10] Among the existing literature, Chinn

---

[8] The regression analysis shows that countries with lower inflation rates have deeper banking systems (results not shown).

[9] The index of constraints on the executive, from the Polity IV database, measures checks and balances on the executive branch of government. It is used as a proxy for the quality of property rights, given that data on the latter are severely constrained in the time-series dimension.

[10] A recent study by Binici, Hutchison, and Schindler (2009) examines in more detail the effects of capital controls on financial flows. Consistent with the findings reported here, they find that the effects of capital controls on equity-like flows (portfolio equity and FDI) are larger than those on debt flows. However, they also differentiate between inflow and outflow controls, based on the dataset in Schindler (2009), and find that outflow controls tend to be more effective in limiting financial flows.

Figure 5.3. Financial Depth and Domestic Financial Sector Liberalization

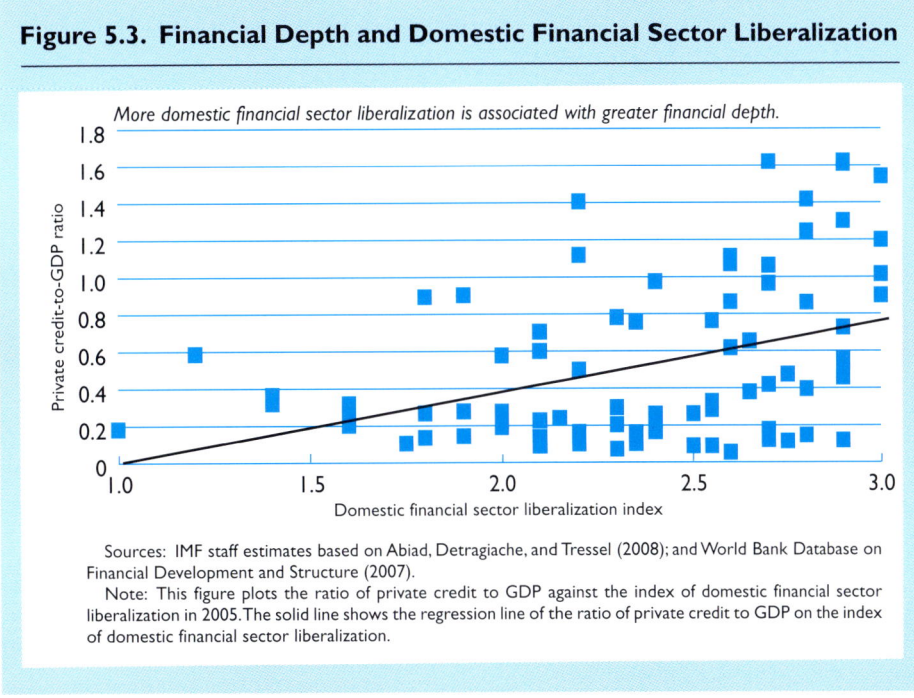

More domestic financial sector liberalization is associated with greater financial depth.

Sources: IMF staff estimates based on Abiad, Detragiache, and Tressel (2008); and World Bank Database on Financial Development and Structure (2007).

Note: This figure plots the ratio of private credit to GDP against the index of domestic financial sector liberalization in 2005. The solid line shows the regression line of the ratio of private credit to GDP on the index of domestic financial sector liberalization.

Table 5.3. Effects of Financial Sector Reforms on Financial Depth

Dependent Variable: Change in Log of Private Credit to GDP (t)	(1)	(2)	(3)
Change in domestic financial sector liberalization index ($t-1$)	0.272*** (0.063)		
Change in banking subindex ($t-1$)		0.233*** (0.058)	
Change in banking subindex excluding supervision ($t-1$)			0.240*** (0.052)
Change in banking supervision subindex ($t-1$)			−0.046* (0.026)
Change in securities subindex ($t-1$)		0.036 (0.032)	0.032 (0.032)
Change in external capital account liberalization index ($t-1$)	0.030* (0.018)	0.031* (0.018)	0.028 (0.018)
Change in log of private credit to GDP ($t-1$)	0.463*** (0.039)	0.463*** (0.039)	0.461*** (0.039)
Observations	2,102	2,102	2,102
R-squared	0.34	0.34	0.34

Sources: IMF staff estimates; Abiad, Detragiache, and Tressel (2008); IMF, *International Financial Statistics*; and World Bank, *World Development Indicators*.

Notes: The table shows regressions of the change in financial depth, measured as the change in the private-credit-to-GDP ratio, on changes of financial sector liberalization indicators. The banking subindex excluding supervision is a simple average of the credit control, interest rate control, privatization, and competition subindices. All specifications were estimated by panel OLS with year fixed effects, using annual data over 1975–2006. Robust standard errors are in parentheses. ***, **, and * denote statistical significance at the 1, 5, and 10 percent level, respectively.

Robustness: Results are robust to the inclusion of the rate of inflation, GDP per capita, real GDP growth, and a dummy for hyperinflation as control variables. The results hold also when the regressions are estimated on the subsample of developing countries.

Box 5.2. Determinants of Financial Development[1]

The role of finance in development and its importance for economic growth have been well established (Levine, 1997 and 2005). A central question is why financial markets are deeper in some countries than in others, and which specific policies might accelerate financial development where it lags behind.

The impetus to reduce the role of the state in financial markets is often attributed to the influential work of McKinnon (1973) and Shaw (1973), who argued that widespread interference by the state in financial markets was responsible for low financial intermediation, especially in developing countries. Examples of interference by the state included low deposit interest rates, high lending interest rates, monopoly power of banks, and concentration of credit in favored sectors and firms. Has financial liberalization borne the fruits of deepening financial systems?

The first figure describes the average behavior of the ratio of private credit to GDP during episodes of significant banking sector reforms. This figure suggests that banking reforms are often accompanied by a deepening of the financial system. However, a more nuanced stylized fact emerges when looking at the evolution over time of the cross-country dispersion of banking sector depth and of the banking reform index (see second figure). Indeed, while the dispersion in the banking reform index has drastically fallen over the past decades, an increase in the dispersion of the ratio of private credit to GDP has taken place, suggesting that banking reforms have not always led to higher financial depth. Possibly related, the recent empirical literature raises the potentially important issue that the impact of financial reforms on financial development may depend on the broader institutional environment (see discussion in main text).

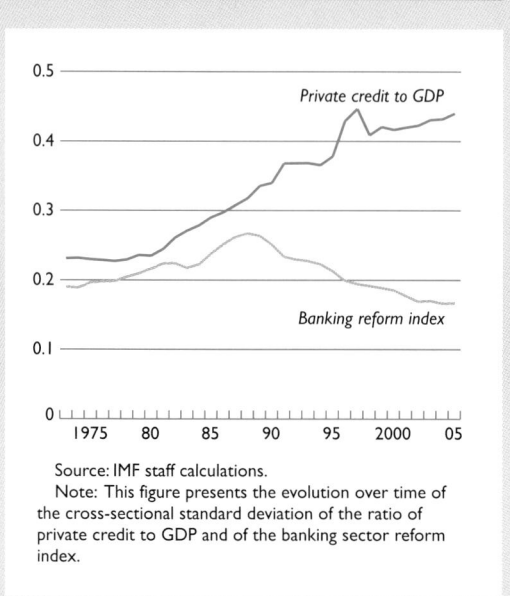

Standard Deviations over Time

Source: IMF staff calculations.
Note: This figure presents the evolution over time of the cross-sectional standard deviation of the ratio of private credit to GDP and of the banking sector reform index.

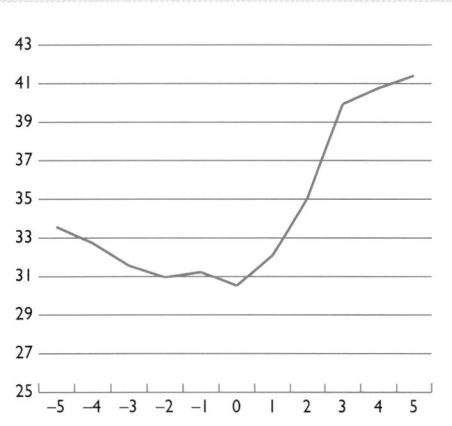

Private Credit to GDP During Banking Reform Episodes
(Mean, in percent)

Source: IMF staff calculations.
Note: This figure presents the average behavior of the ratio of private credit to GDP around episodes of intense banking sector reforms (five years before the reform to five years following the reform). Episodes of intense banking sector reforms are defined as years when the change in the banking reform index is greater than the top quartile of the distribution of changes.

To ascertain the relationship between banking reforms and financial deepening, we consider a general dynamic autoregressive distributed lag model linking financial development y_{it} in country i at date t, to the index of banking reforms I_{it}, and a vector of macroeconomic control variables X_{it} with year and country fixed effects. This specification allows us to analyze the dynamic effects of banking reforms. Specifically, we estimate the specification as an error-correction model, assuming a maximum number of lags N = 5.

Estimating the dynamic specification as an error-correction model allows to go around the problem that the banking sector liberalization index is highly persistent within countries. Indeed, when we run a simple OLS regression with country and year fixed effects, the coefficient on the first lag of the index is 0.86. This high persistence may, in practice, introduce multicollinearity problems. Therefore, we rearrange the equation to estimate a relationship between the (log) change in financial development and changes in the banking sector liberalization index ΔI_{t-k} (the formal derivation is in Tressel and Detragiache, 2008). In this error-correction specification, the level of the index appears only once, with N lags, and the change in the index ΔI_{t-k} measures a banking sector reform occurring at date $t-k$:

What Explains the Lack of Sustained Effect of Reforms on Financial Depth in Developing Countries?

Institutions Sample	Strong Property Rights (1)	Weak Property Rights (2)	Strong Creditor Rights (3)	Weak Creditor Rights (4)	Civil Law (5)	Strong Banking Supervision[1] (6)	Weak Banking Supervision[1] (7)
Banking reform index (t–5)	0.132*** (0.045)	–0.019 (0.089)	0.09 (0.060)	–0.017 (0.050)	0.095 (0.071)	–0.043 (0.05)	0.016 (0.01)
Change in banking reform index	0.051 (0.064)	0.124 (0.13)	0.102 (0.086)	0.01 (0.102)	0.063 (0.135)	–0.03 (0.07)	0.011 (0.02)
Change in banking reform index (t–1)	0.170** (0.065)	0.065 (0.102)	0.128* (0.066)	0.039 (0.108)	0.046 (0.078)	–0.051 (0.06)	0.059*** (0.02)
Change in banking reform index (t–2)	0.115** (0.049)	0.166 (0.107)	0.103* (0.060)	0.142 (0.093)	0.105 (0.068)	–0.024 (0.05)	0.042*** (0.02)
Change in banking reform index (t–3)	0.096 (0.062)	–0.029 (0.129)	0.079 (0.073)	–0.053 (0.094)	0.171* (0.089)	–0.067 (0.06)	0.009 (0.02)
Change in banking reform index (t–4)	0.157** (0.063)	–0.058 (0.121)	0.076 (0.063)	–0.027 (0.107)	–0.002 (0.109)	–0.059 (0.06)	0.003 (0.02)
Long-run effect	1.303** (0.599)	–0.206 (0.299)	0.741 (0.509)	–0.150 (0.439)	0.872 (0.649)	0.278 (0.171)	0.079 (0.108)
Observations	911	676	1,008	650	589	246	1,511
R-squared	0.6	0.47	0.52	0.49	0.42	0.81	0.38

Notes: This table presents regressions of the error correction specification (1). The dependent variable is the log of the annual change in the private credit-to-GDP ratio, and the right-hand side variables include lags of the log change in private credit to GDP, and the log of private credit to GDP, lagged five times. Key explanatory variables are the changes in the banking reform index, from t to $t-4$, and the level of the banking reform index, lagged five times. All regressions include country and year fixed effects, as well as five lags of inflation and of GDP per capita, as control variables. The sample is split using the median of the relevant variable, unless otherwise indicated.

Robust standard errors in parentheses, observations are clustered by country. ***, **, and * denote statistical significance at the 1, 5, and 10 percent level, respectively.

[1] In these columns, the banking reform index excludes the banking supervision subindex which is instead used to split the sample. The "strong supervision" group includes all country-year pairs for which the supervision index takes one of the two top values at date $t-5$, and the "weak supervision" group is the complement.

$$\Delta y_{it} = \alpha_0 + \sum_{j=1}^{N-1} \lambda_j \cdot \Delta y_{i,t-j} + \lambda_N \cdot y_{i,t-N} + \sum_{j=0}^{N-1} \mu_j$$

$$\cdot \Delta I_{i,t-j} + \sum_{j=0}^{N-1} \theta_j \cdot \Delta X_{i,t-j} + \mu_N \cdot I_{i,t-N} + \theta_N$$

$$\cdot X_{i,t-N} + \varepsilon_{it}. \qquad (1)$$

In this model, the cumulative direct effect of a reform episode occurring at date $t-i$ on financial deepening of date of date t is given by μ_N. As a result of persistence in the levels of financial development, there are also *indirect* effects of past reforms on the current financial deepening through their effects on lagged values of the dependent variable. The long-run direct and indirect effects of financial reforms and the other control variables on financial development can be easily obtained from the coefficients of equation (1). Specifically, the long-run effect of financial reforms is equal to

$$-\frac{\mu_N}{\lambda_N} = -\frac{\sum_{u=0}^{N} \gamma_u}{\sum_{u=1}^{N} \beta_u - 1}. \qquad (2)$$

The long-run effect of the control variables on financial development is

$$-\frac{\theta_N}{\lambda_N} = -\frac{\sum_{u=0}^{N} \varphi_u}{\sum_{u=1}^{N} \beta_u - 1}. \qquad (3)$$

Finally, the error term v_{it} is assumed to be independently distributed. At a minimum of robustness, standard errors are clustered by country to allow for heteroskedasticity and possible serial correlation in the error term.

V STRUCTURAL REFORMS AND ECONOMIC GROWTH

> **Box 5.2 (concluded)**
>
> To test the importance of the institutional environment in shaping the impact of banking reforms, we split the sample according to various institutional characteristics (see table on previous page).[2] We find that banking sector reforms have a sustained impact on financial development only in environments in which property rights are well protected.[3] These results suggest that protection of property rights is complementary to financial reforms.
>
> A possible interpretation is that, in countries where expropriation is easy, financial reforms reduce the role of the state in the financial sector only on paper, while powerful elites continue to be able to divert financial resources to their own benefit, ultimately undermining the effectiveness of market mechanisms. Also, in these countries private sector business initiatives from groups that are not politically powerful may be constantly threatened with expropriation by more powerful groups. As a result, such initiatives may not find financing from sound and profit-maximizing banks even if they are economically viable. Thus, with weak property rights protection, privatized banks operating in a competitive market may be able to lend profitably only to well-connected groups or the government.
>
> ---
> [1]This box draws upon Tressel and Detragiache (2008).
> [2]When estimated on the complete sample of countries, or on the sample of developing countries, the dynamic model shows that the effects of banking reforms on financial depth are, on average, not sustained beyond the first two years following a reform.
> [3]The degree of protection against the risk of expropriation is proxied by the Polity IV index of constraints on the executive. Results are robust when using other measures of property right protection.

and Ito (2006) focus on the effect of removing restrictions on international financial transactions (capital account liberalization) on various indicators of financial development. They find that capital account liberalization leads to stock market development only in countries with sufficiently developed legal systems, while the effect is negative elsewhere.

To gain further perspective on the channels through which domestic financial sector reform underpins growth, we consider the possible allocative effects across different manufacturing sectors that result in efficiency gains at a macroeconomic level. As argued by Rajan and Zingales (1998), it is expected that liberalizing the financial sector should have particularly favorable effects on the growth of sectors that rely relatively heavily on external finance for their investment and growth. Those may be the sectors that require large up-front investments, that have greater growth opportunities, or that are more adversely affected by credit rationing (Fisman and Love, 2004; and Bernanke and Gertler, 1989).

The differential effect of financial reforms on manufacturing output growth is estimated as an interaction between the banking reform index and a measure of external dependence on finance. The measure of external dependence on finance is defined as the share of investment that is not financed by retained earnings. This share is computed for U.S. manufacturing industries over 1980–99. As explained by Rajan and Zingales (1998), the rationale for using U.S. data is that U.S. firms are the least likely to be financially

Table 5.4. Foreign Direct Investment Inflows and Financial Sector Reforms

Dependent Variable: log FDI/GDP(t)	Domestic Financial Sector Liberalization (1)	Banking Subindex (2)	Securities Subindex (3)	External Capital Account Liberalization (4)
Liberalization index (t–1)	0.462	0.261	0.471*	0.534***
	(0.432)	(0.379)	(0.254)	(0.144)
Observations	1,844	1,844	1,844	1,844
Number of countries	81	81	81	81
Adjusted R-squared	0.63	0.63	0.63	0.64

Sources: IMF staff estimates based on IMF, *International Financial Statistics*; Penn World Tables version 6.2; and World Bank, *World Development Indicators*.
Notes: The table shows regressions of inward FDI, measured as the log of FDI to GDP, on financial sector liberalization indicators. Each regression includes controls for the growth of real per capita GDP, the level of development (proxied by the lagged level of real GDP per capita), market size (proxied by the lagged level of real GDP), and inflation. All regressions were estimated by panel OLS and include country and year fixed effects, using annual data over 1961–2006. Robust standard errors, clustered at the country-year level, are in parentheses. ***, **, and * denote statistical significance at the 1, 5, and 10 percent level, respectively.

Table 5.5. The Differential Effects of Financial Reforms in Manufacturing Industries

Dependent Variable: Growth of Sectoral Output	Financial Reforms			
	(1)	(2)	(3)	(4)
External financial dependence * banking subindex (t–1)	0.009*** (0.002)	0.005* (0.003)	0.009*** (0.002)	
External financial dependence * banking subindex (t–1) Above median constraint on the executive				0.013 (5.41)***
External financial dependence * banking subindex (t–1) Below median constraint on the executive				–0.0005 (0.11)
External financial dependence * GDP per capita (t–1)		6.50E–07** (3.03E–07)		
External financial dependence * log days to enforce contracts			–0.012 (–0.005)	
Log output share (t–1)	0.001 (0.001)	0.001 (0.001)	0.002 (0.001)	0.001 (0.60)
Observations	35,619	34,878	35,619	32,944
Number of countries	62	62	62	60
R-squared	0.02	0.02	0.02	0.02

Sources: United Nations Industrial Development Organization (2006); Abiad, Detragiache, and Tressel (2008); World Bank, *World Development Indicators*; and IMF staff estimates. The sectoral measure of dependence on external finance is from Kroszner, Laeven, and Klingebiel (2007).

Notes: The dependent variable is sectoral output growth of manufacturing industries over 1974–2003. The differential effects of a banking reform on sectoral output growth is estimated by interacting the measure of external dependence on finance with the reform index, following the approach of Rajan and Zingales (1998). Results are robust when controlling for the overall level of development (column 2), for the quality of contract enforcement (column 3), and hold when using the index of domestic financial reforms instead of the banking subindex. Regressions include industry dummies and a full set of country-specific time dummies. Standard errors are robust to heterogeneity and observations are clustered at the country-year level. R^2 is a partial R-squared after netting out the country-specific time dummies. ***, **, and * denote statistical significance at the 1, 5, and 10 percent level, respectively.

constrained for regulatory reasons, and therefore the share of externally financed investment is more likely to capture industry technological characteristics rather than inefficiencies of the financial system. Regressions include a full set of country-specific time dummies that account for the effects of any possible macroeconomic factors on manufacturing output growth, as well as industry-specific dummies that account for industry-specific trends in output.

The results of Table 5.5 show that banking sector liberalization disproportionately increases the growth of the sectors that have a relatively higher need for external finance. This is consistent with the finding that financial development fosters an efficient use of resources at the aggregate level (Beck, Levine, and Loayza, 2000). The estimated effects, moreover, are large: a one standard deviation increase in the banking liberalization index raises the annual growth rate of sectors with a high dependence on external finance (top 75th percentile of the distribution), relative to the growth rate of sectors with a low dependence on external finance (bottom 25th percentile of the distribution), by nearly 1 percentage point. These results are not explained by differences in GDP per capita (column (2)), nor by differences in the quality of private contract enforcement (column (3)).

Column (4), however, shows that banking sector liberalization improves the allocation of capital only in countries with a good protection of property rights. In other countries, the allocative effect of banking reforms across manufacturing industries becomes economically and statistically insignificant, suggesting that the degree of protection of property rights can be a constraint on the effectiveness of financial reforms. The importance of property rights for development and growth has been recently emphasized by Acemoglu and Johnson (2005). Following North (1981), these authors argue that the social, economic, legal, and political organizations of a society (its broad "institutions") are primary determinants of economic performance (Acemoglu, Johnson, and Robinson, 2001 and 2002). These results are consistent with recent papers that have found that property rights also have a direct differential effect on sectors according to the degree of intangibility of assets (Claessens and Laeven, 2003) or to the degree of technological advancement (Aghion, Alesina, and Trebbi, 2007).

As argued above, the effects of structural reforms on per capita income are spread out through time, as growth accelerates for a number of years in response to liberalization. Is this longer-run growth impact internalized in forward-looking variables that should, in principle,

V STRUCTURAL REFORMS AND ECONOMIC GROWTH

Table 5.6. Financial Sector Reforms and Foreign Currency Bond Ratings

Dependent Variable: Foreign Currency Bond Ratings (t)	Domestic Financial Sector Liberalization (1)	Securities Subindex (2)	Banking Subindex (3)	External Capital Account Liberalization (4)
Corporate ratings				
Liberalization index (t)	13.370***	9.878***	11.817***	4.535***
	(2.215)	(2.929)	(2.022)	(1.187)
Sovereign rating (t)	1.286***	1.123***	1.179***	0.754***
	(0.132)	(0.217)	(0.112)	(0.078)
Liberalization index interacted with sovereign rating (t)	−0.943***	−0.683***	−0.833***	−0.330***
	(0.149)	(0.226)	(0.129)	(0.089)
Observations	2,032	2,032	2,032	2,032
R-squared	0.69	0.68	0.69	0.67
Bank ratings				
Liberalization index (t)	12.027***	8.209**	9.809***	6.705***
	(3.392)	(3.235)	(3.109)	(1.292)
Sovereign rating (t)	0.950***	0.942***	0.886***	0.896***
	(0.134)	(0.224)	(0.119)	(0.088)
Liberalization index interacted with sovereign rating (t)	−0.403**	−0.225	−0.325**	−0.261**
	(0.176)	(0.236)	(0.163)	(0.110)
Observations	694	694	694	694
R-squared	0.86	0.85	0.85	0.85
Sovereign ratings				
Reform ($t-1$)	−0.193	−1.007***	0.130	0.851***
	(0.308)	(0.288)	(0.269)	(0.178)
Observations	887	887	887	887
R-squared	0.97	0.98	0.97	0.98

Sources: IMF staff estimates based on IMF, *International Financial Statistics*; World Bank, *World Development Indicators*; and Standard & Poor's.

Notes: The table shows regressions of foreign currency bond ratings on financial sector liberalization indicators. Bond ratings were mapped into numerical values ranging from 1 to 21, with 21 representing the highest (AAA) rating. Each regression also includes as control variables: time fixed effects, inflation, real per capita GDP, and real per capita GDP growth averaged over the previous five years. For corporate ratings, additional controls include sector fixed effects, current account balance, GDP growth volatility, and the ratios of earnings before interest and taxes (EBIT) to assets and to interest expense, retained earnings/assets, working capital/assets, total assets, and equity/(equity+debt). For bank ratings, additional controls include sector fixed effects, current account balance, GDP growth volatility, equity/assets, loan growth, operation expenses/assets, net interest margin, deposits/assets, and total assets. For sovereign ratings, additional controls include country dummies, external balance, fiscal balance, default history, and external debt. All regressions were estimated by panel OLS, using annual data over 1995–2005. Robust standard errors, clustered by country-year in the corporate and bank rating regressions, are in parentheses. ***, **, and * denote statistical significance at the 1, 5, and 10 percent level, respectively.

Robustness: The regressions in the table are estimated with contemporaneous control variables (except for the sovereign ratings regressions); results are broadly similar when controls are lagged one period. The results also hold when the sample is restricted to industrial countries or emerging markets, and, in the corporate ratings regressions, when liberalization firms in the tradable and nontradable sectors are considered separately. Results are also robust to using alternative external capital account liberalization indices, including those accounting for differences between restrictions on residents and nonresidents (Quinn, 1997) and those accounting for different asset categories and inflow versus outflow controls (Schindler, 2009).

anticipate such effects? To assess this issue, the analysis now focuses on credit ratings, which should improve if reforms elicit persistent changes in the solvency of corporations and banks, beyond contemporaneous effects on determinants of repayment probability—such as the ratio of earnings to total assets and debt-equity ratios.[11] The empirical results are very much in line with the hypothesis that credit ratings anticipate the persistent beneficial effects of structural reforms on the corporate sector (Table 5.6). Specifically, an improvement in the domestic financial sector reform index from the 25th to the 75th percentile of the distribution raises corporate credit ratings by almost 1½ points and banks' credit ratings by almost 4 points—equivalent to 40–80 percent

---
[11]Equity prices should also incorporate relevant information about the impact of structural reforms on the solvency/health/profitability of domestic firms. The empirical association of equity prices with structural reform indices is weak, however, likely reflecting the very different volatility properties of the two sets of variables.

of the sample difference in credit ratings between the average corporation/bank in high-income and middle-income countries. The impact of capital account liberalization on credit ratings is almost as large, reflecting also its positive effect on sovereign ratings, which lifts the sovereign ceiling on private ratings. Given that credit ratings are highly correlated with bond spreads, this evidence suggests that financial sector reforms reduce the cost of credit of banks and corporations, and improve their access to international credit markets.[12]

Real Sector Reforms

This section examines how real sector reforms—those relating to international trade, agriculture, and the telecommunications and electricity sectors—affect growth. The conventional wisdom (based, for instance, on the studies by Krueger, Schiff, and Valdés, 1992; Sachs and Warner, 1995; and Dollar and Kraay, 2004) is that there is a positive association between real sector reforms—especially trade liberalization—and income growth, but a broad examination of the cross-country evidence is still missing to underpin this conclusion.

The event study analysis based on growth accelerations/decelerations discussed in the previous subsection generally supports the view that real sector reforms anticipate growth spurts, while reversals foreshadow decelerations (Figure 5.4). Specifically, in the run-up to growth upbreaks, economies have already reduced tariff rates—with the tariff-based trade liberalization index above the country-specific average in the top panel of Figure 5.4. In addition, reductions in trade-related current account restrictions and in the pervasiveness of agricultural sector restrictions (e.g., export marketing boards) are in evidence about three years before a growth upbreak, and continue thereafter (middle and bottom panels of Figure 5.4). Conversely, growth downbreaks seem to be anticipated by an illiberal tariff regime and reversals of current account liberalization, but no significant change in agricultural liberalization (although reversals are apparent once the downturn is in train).

Econometric evidence corroborates the event-study analysis, with panel growth regressions indicating a statistically significant impact of real sector reforms on economic growth, after controlling for a standard set of growth covariates (Table 5.7). Agricultural liberalization and reductions in restrictions on trade-related current account transactions yield the largest growth benefits. An improvement in the corresponding indices from the 25th to the 75th percentile—consistent, for example, with the changes in agricultural liberalization achieved in Poland in the late 1980s and current account liberalization achieved in Peru at roughly the same time—is estimated to increase long-run income per capita by about 40–50 percent.[13] The effects are somewhat stronger over the sample of low- and middle-income countries, in line with the greater weight of the farm sector in such economies, and the role of exports in the development strategies of a number of nonindustrial countries. Finally, with respect to telecommunications and electricity deregulation, while previous studies for industrial countries have found significant effects on productivity growth (Nicoletti and Scarpetta, 2003), the broad cross-country evidence fails to uncover much impact, likely reflecting the late adoption of these reforms in developing countries.

Next, Table 5.8 reports alternative regression results from a specification based on the neo-Schumpeterian approach (discussed in Box 5.1), in which each liberalization index enters the regression both directly and interacted with the country's "income gap" relative to the world output frontier, as in Table 5.2. The results imply that, in addition to domestic financial liberalization, some real structural reforms also speed up income convergence. Specifically, liberalizing the agricultural sector and the current account both help to close the income gap relative to frontier countries (proxied here by the level of output in the United States).

Taken together, the results from the alternative "income-gap" approach (Tables 5.2 and 5.8) show that some reforms, namely of domestic finance, agriculture, and the current account, can speed up the convergence of a country's income toward the levels prevailing in the world's richest economies. It is important to note here that these results are consistent with the results from the neoclassical specification (Tables 5.1 and 5.7), which showed that the growth effects of agriculture and current account reforms (among real sector reforms) and of banking reform (among financial sector reforms) are larger in low- and middle-income countries.

What can be said about the channels through which real sector reforms affect growth? A starting point, given the established linkage between growth and trade (e.g., Frankel and Romer, 1999), is to examine the association between trade liberalization and de facto trade openness (import- and export-to-GDP shares), which indeed is robustly positive (Table 5.9). In line with the results in Table 5.6, the index based on current account liberalization has a larger effect on trade flows than the index based on tariffs, with an increase in the current account reform index from the 25th to the 75th percen-

---

[12]Focusing on corporate foreign currency bond ratings as a dependent variable, and using a difference-in-difference approach, Prati, Schindler, and Valenzuela (forthcoming) argue that capital account restrictions have a particularly strong effect on firms in the nontradables sector, that is, on firms that cannot easily generate foreign currency out of their regular business activities.

[13]About half the long-run effects are achieved within 20 years, and 20 percent in the first 5 years.

V STRUCTURAL REFORMS AND ECONOMIC GROWTH

Figure 5.4. Growth Breaks and Real Sector Reforms

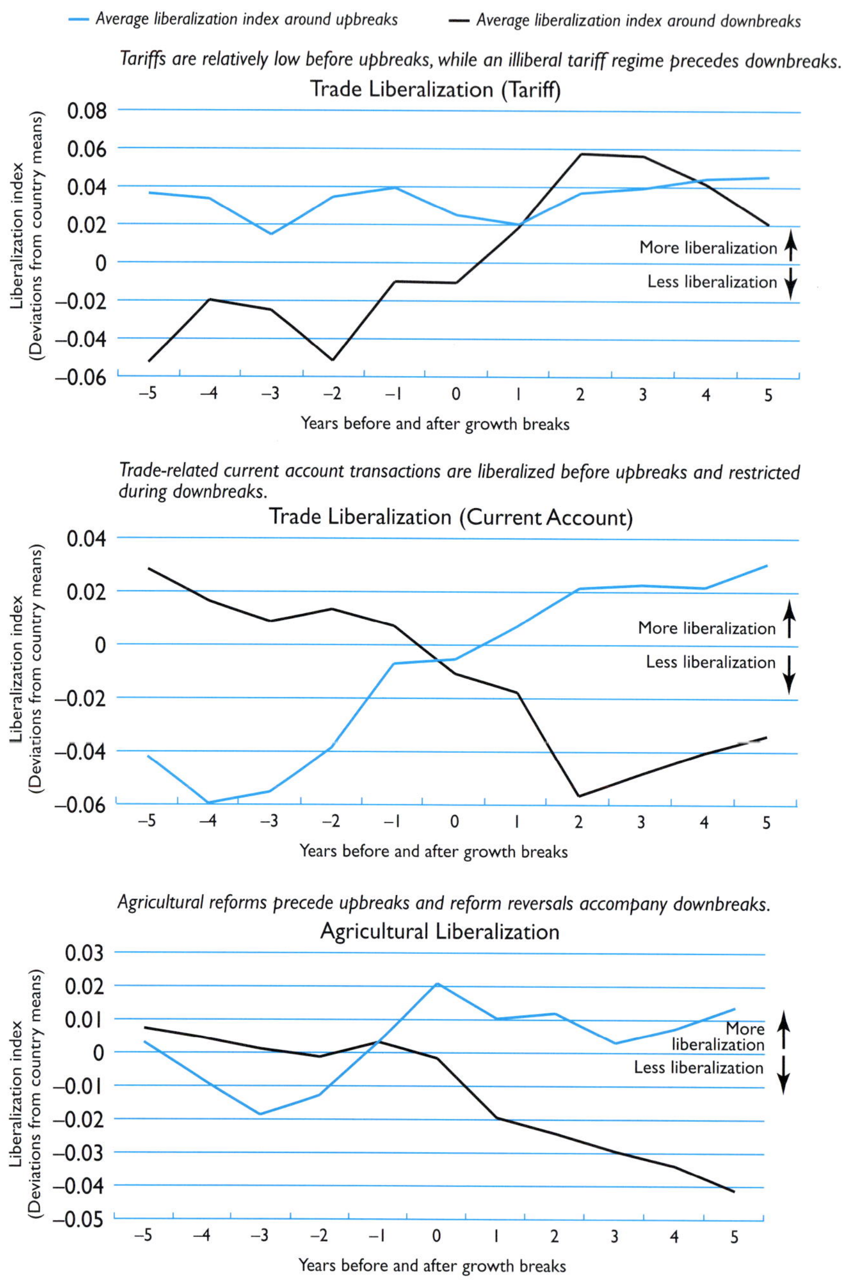

— Average liberalization index around upbreaks   — Average liberalization index around downbreaks

Tariffs are relatively low before upbreaks, while an illiberal tariff regime precedes downbreaks.

Trade Liberalization (Tariff)

Trade-related current account transactions are liberalized before upbreaks and restricted during downbreaks.

Trade Liberalization (Current Account)

Agricultural reforms precede upbreaks and reform reversals accompany downbreaks.

Agricultural Liberalization

Source: IMF staff estimates based on Penn World Tables version 6.2.
Note: The figures plot average liberalization indices for the period beginning five years before a growth break (year 0 on the horizontal axis) and ending five years after the growth break. The plots capture the within-country evolution of the liberalization indices obtained from a panel regression of each index on country fixed effects (to remove country averages) and year fixed effects (to remove global trends). As a result, the zero value on the vertical axis corresponds to the sample average of the liberalization indices for the countries considered. The number of countries used to compute each average varies across indices in line with data availability. No figure is shown for the case of telecommunications and electricity reform, because there are not enough growth breaks after 1990, the year that liberalizations in this sector generally begin.

Table 5.7. Growth Regression Results: Real Sector Reforms (1)

Dependent Variable: logGDP(t) – logGDP(t–1)	Trade Liberalization (Tariff) (1)	Trade Liberalization (Current Account) (2)	Agricultural Liberalization (3)	Telecommunications and Electricity Liberalization (4)
Entire sample				
Liberalization index (t–1)	0.022***	0.034***	0.028***	–0.001
	(0.009)	(0.007)	(0.007)	(0.008)
Long-run income effect: 25–75 percentile improvement	0.135***	0.425***	0.519***	–0.001
	(0.054)	(0.094)	(0.132)	(0.019)
Observations	2,616	1,719	2,310	2,411
Number of countries	118	58	94	92
Adjusted R-squared	0.13	0.16	0.13	0.13
Low- and middle-income group				
Liberalization index (t–1)	0.024***	0.042***	0.034***	–0.009
	(0.010)	(0.010)	(0.008)	(0.013)
Long-run income effect: 25–75 percentile improvement	0.131***	0.438***	0.581***	0.000
	(0.055)	(0.107)	(0.139)	(0.000)
Observations	1,802	1,026	1,653	1,618
Number of countries	97	41	72	72
Adjusted R-squared	0.11	0.14	0.13	0.12

Sources: IMF staff estimates based on IMF, *International Financial Statistics*; Penn World Tables version 6.2; and World Bank, *World Development Indicators*.

Notes: The table shows regressions of annual growth in real GDP per capita on real sector liberalization indicators. The regressions are estimated for the entire country sample and for the group of low- and middle-income countries (see Appendix Table A1). Each regression includes as controls the lagged level of real GDP per capita, an indicator variable for democratic regimes, the level of terms of trade, and the level of tertiary school enrollment. The long-run income effect captures the estimated change in the steady-state level of GDP per capita resulting from an improvement in the liberalization index from the 25th to the 75th percentile. All specifications were estimated by panel OLS with country and year fixed effects, using annual data over 1960–2005. Robust standard errors are in parentheses. The standard errors on the long-run effects are calculated with the delta method. ***, **, and * denote statistical significance at the 1, 5, and 10 percent level, respectively.

Robustness: To address possible endogeneity, all specifications were also estimated by panel 2SLS with country fixed effects and five-year lags of the liberalization index as instrument. The results are robust to this alternative specification. Most results hold also in regressions estimated on five-year nonoverlapping intervals with growth rates over a five-year period regressed on five-year lags of each liberalization index.

tile of the sample distribution yielding an increase in trade shares of 10–15 percentage points of GDP (last row of Table 5.9).

Apart from the trade channel, resource reallocation in response to a move to a more market-based price structure is likely to be a key driver of growth following trade reforms. The aggregate impact of trade reforms has been well established (see Berg and Krueger, 2003; and Edwards, 1993, for a discussion of earlier literature). Theories of trade under imperfect competition indeed show how trade enhances growth through the import of new varieties of intermediate inputs in which technical knowledge is embodied, and predict that lowering the cost of imported inputs faced by domestic firms is likely to increase their productivity (Romer, 1986; and Grossman and Helpman, 1990). These theories imply that trade liberalization (in particular a reduction in tariffs) is likely to particularly benefit sectors relying relatively more on imports of intermediate goods in production.

The findings of recent microeconometric and country studies confirm the importance of a trade channel going through the imports of intermediate goods (Pavcnik, 2002; Edwards and Lawrence, 2006; Amiti and Konings, 2005; and Broda, Greenfield, and Weinstein, 2006). The hypothesis is that trade reforms—such as a reduction in import tariffs—should disproportionately foster growth in sectors in which a country has a comparative advantage and that, for technological reasons, depend on traded intermediate goods in the production process. For each three-digit manufacturing sector, we construct a measure of intensity of the use of traded inputs, defined as the share of imported inputs in the total value added of intermediate inputs, averaged across a large number of countries.

Table 5.10 shows that trade liberalization—measured by a simple index of average tariffs (column 1), or by an index of restrictions on the current account (column 2)—disproportionately improve the growth of sectors

V STRUCTURAL REFORMS AND ECONOMIC GROWTH

Table 5.8. Growth Regression Results: Real Sector Reforms (2)

Dependent Variable: logGDP(t) − logGDP(t−1)	Trade Liberalization (Tariff) (1)	Trade Liberalization (Current Account) (2)	Agricultural Liberalization (3)	Telecommunications and Electricity Liberalization (4)
Entire sample				
Liberalization index (t−1)	0.022***	0.049***	0.043***	0.011
	(0.0128)	(0.0115)	(0.0099)	(0.0135)
Liberalization index * (GDPj / GDPus) (t−1)	−0.028	−0.054**	−0.045**	−0.130
	(0.0369)	(0.0231)	(0.0231)	(0.0176)
Observations	2,616	1,719	2,310	2,411
Number of countries	118	58	94	92
Adjusted R-squared	0.12	0.15	0.13	0.12

Sources: IMF staff estimates based on IMF, *International Financial Statistics*; Penn World Tables version 6.2; and World Bank, *World Development Indicators*.

Notes: The table shows regressions of annual growth in real GDP per capita on real sector liberalization indicators. The regressions are estimated for the entire country sample (see Appendix Table A1). Each regression includes as controls the lagged ratio of the level of real GDP per capita in country j to the level of real GDP in the United States, an indicator variable for democratic regimes, the level of terms of trade, and the level of tertiary school enrollment. All specifications were estimated by panel OLS with country and year fixed effects, using annual data over 1960–2005. Robust standard errors are in parentheses. ***, **, and * denote statistical significance at the 1, 5, and 10 percent level, respectively.

Robustness: To address possible endogeneity, all specifications were also estimated by panel 2SLS with country fixed effects and five-year lags of the liberalization index as instrument. The results are robust to this alternative specification. Most results hold also in regressions estimated on five-year nonoverlapping intervals with growth rates over a five-year period regressed on five-year lags of each liberalization index.

that have a relatively higher dependence on imported intermediate goods in production. The estimated coefficient of column 1 implies that a one standard deviation improvement in the average tariff index (i.e., a reduction in average tariff rates of about 15 percentage points) raises relative annual growth in sectors using imported inputs intensively by about 0.1 percentage point. Like financial sector reforms, however, trade reforms effectively improve the growth of sectors dependent on imported intermediate inputs only when the protection of property rights is strong enough, in particular in developing countries (columns 3 and 4).

Like financial sector reforms, real sector reforms also have persistent effects that are anticipated in such forward-looking variables as credit ratings. Results reported in Table 5.11 suggest that both measures of trade liberalization significantly improve the credit ratings of domestic firms, controlling for other potential determinants of repayment probability. A reform, for example, that increases the index of current account liberalization from the 25th to the 75th percentile of the sample distribution is associated with an increase in average corporate credit ratings equivalent to about 20 percent of the sample difference in credit ratings between high- and middle-income countries. Moreover, the total effect approximately doubles if one takes into account that corporate ratings are capped by sovereign ratings, and that the latter are also improved by current account liberalization.

The positive impact of trade reforms on credit ratings is an important example of a favorable real sector and financial sector linkage following structural reform, with the increased efficiency brought about by real sector reforms fostering improved access to credit/investment financing for domestic firms. Such favorable real sector and financial sector linkages are also apparent from the impact of current account reform on financial depth (Table 5.12, second row/second column), and the effects of telecommunications and electricity reforms on FDI (Table 5.13, fourth column).

Table 5.9. Trade Reforms and Export- and Import-to-GDP Share

	Exports/GDP		Imports/GDP	
Dependent Variable: Annual Ratio of Exports (Imports) to GDP (t)	Trade liberalization (tariff) (1)	Trade liberalization (current account) (2)	Trade liberalization (tariff) (3)	Trade Liberalization (current account) (4)
Trade liberalization index ($t-1$)	1.754*** (0.556)	2.349*** (0.452)	1.397*** (0.487)	2.659*** (0.423)
Exports/GDP ($t-1$)	0.835*** (0.022)	0.881*** (0.016)		
Imports/GDP ($t-1$)			0.855*** (0.014)	0.897*** (0.014)
Trading partners' income growth ($t-1$)	0.104** (0.049)	0.193*** (0.057)		
Domestic income growth ($t-1$)			0.068** (0.028)	0.078*** (0.025)
Long-run effect: 25–75 percentile improvement in the trade liberalization index	2.911*** (0.741)	11.106*** (2.043)	2.637*** (0.905)	14.510*** (2.321)
Observations	3,618	2,091	3,777	2,290
Number of countries	140	58	140	58
Adjusted R-squared	0.70	0.80	0.74	0.83

Sources: IMF staff estimates based on IMF, *International Financial Statistics*; and World Bank, *World Development Indicators*.

Notes: The table shows regressions of the share of exports and imports of goods and services in GDP on indices of trade reform, separately for the index based on tariffs and the index based on current account restrictions. The control variables include domestic GDP growth (for imports) and trading partners' GDP growth (for exports); all variables are lagged one year to avoid potential problems of endogeneity. In addition, all regressions include the lagged dependent variable to control for persistence in export- and import-to-GDP shares. The long-run effect is the long-term change in terms of GDP shares resulting from an increase in the openness index from the 25th to the 75th percentile of the in-sample distribution. All specifications are estimated by ordinary least squared regression with country fixed effects, using annual data over 1968–2006. Robust standard errors are in parentheses. The standard errors on the long-term effects are calculated with the delta method. ***, **, and * denote statistical significance at the 1, 5, and 10 percent level, respectively.

Robustness: The results are robust to additional controls used in the related literature, including terms of trade shocks and fiscal balance as a share of GDP; however, the inclusion of these variables reduces considerably the sample size.

V STRUCTURAL REFORMS AND ECONOMIC GROWTH

Table 5.10. The Differential Effects of Trade Reforms in Manufacturing Industries

Dependent Variable: Growth of Sectoral Output	Trade Reforms			(Developing countries only)
	(1)	(2)	(3)	(4)
Intensity imported inputs (exporters) * index average tariff (t–1)	0.033*** (0.006)			
Intensity imported inputs (exporters) * index average tariff (t–1) Above median constraint on the executive			0.033 (5.81)***	0.022 (1.87)*
Intensity imported inputs (exporters) * index average tariff (t–1) Below median constraint on the executive			0.034 (2.72)***	0.014 (0.59)
Intensity imported inputs (exporters) * index current account restrictions (t–1)		0.027*** (0.005)		
External financial dependence * banking subindex (t–1)	0.013*** (0.003)	0.008 (0.0023)		
External financial dependence * banking subindex (t–1) Above median constraint on the executive			0.015 (5.87)***	0.018 (4.20)***
External financial dependence * banking subindex (t–1) Below median constraint on the executive			0.001 (0.33)	–0.004 (0.68)
Log output share (t–1)	0.001 (0.001)	–0.00004 (0.0014)	0.001 (0.45)	–0.001 (0.39)
Observations	32,770	30,715	31,430	18,165
Number of countries	60	52	57	37
R-squared	0.02	0.02	0.02	0.01

Sources: United Nations Industrial Development Organization (2006); Abiad, Detragiache, and Tressel (2008); World Bank, *World Development Indicators*; and IMF staff estimates. The sectoral measure of dependence on external finance is from Kroszner, Laeven, and Klingebiel (2007).

Notes: The dependent variable is annual sectoral output growth of manufacturing industries over 1974–2003. The differential effects of a reform on sectoral output growth is estimated by interacting a sectoral characteristic with the reform index. The differential effect of trade reforms is estimated as an interaction between the trade index and a measure of intensity of use of imported intermediate inputs. Industry dummies and a full set of country-specific time dummies are included in the regressions. Standard errors are robust to heterogeneity and observations are clustered at the country-year level. R-squared is a partial R-squared after netting out the country-specific time dummies. ***, **, and * denote statistical significance at the 1, 5, and 10 percent level, respectively.

Table 5.11. Real Sector Reforms and Foreign Currency Bond Ratings

Dependent Variable: Foreign Currency Bond Ratings (t)	Trade Liberalization (Tariff) (1)	Trade Liberalization (Current Account) (2)
Corporate ratings		
Liberalization index (t)	9.017*	8.874***
	(5.426)	(1.468)
Sovereign rating (t)	1.463***	1.044***
	(0.377)	(0.100)
Liberalization index interacted with sovereign rating (t)	−1.087**	−0.678***
	(0.443)	(0.112)
Observations	2,032	2,010
R-squared	0.68	0.68
Bank ratings		
Liberalization index (t)	32.004***	2.442
	(6.611)	(1.503)
Sovereign rating (t)	2.647***	0.588***
	(0.458)	(0.105)
Liberalization index interacted with sovereign rating (t)	−2.227***	0.129
	(0.521)	(0.127)
Observations	707	674
R-squared	0.84	0.86
Sovereign ratings		
Reform (t−1)	−2.339***	1.336***
	(0.830)	(0.367)
Observations	963	736
R-squared	0.98	0.98

Sources: IMF staff estimates based on IMF, *International Financial Statistics*; World Bank, *World Development Indicators*; and Standard & Poor's.

Notes: The table shows regressions of foreign currency bond ratings on trade liberalization indicators. Bond ratings were mapped into numerical values ranging from 1 to 21, with 21 representing the highest (AAA) rating. Each regression also includes as control variables: time fixed effects, inflation, real per capita GDP, and real per capita GDP growth averaged over the previous five years. For corporate ratings, additional controls include sector fixed effects, current account balance, GDP growth volatility, and the ratios of earnings before interest and taxes (EBIT) to assets and to interest expense, retained earnings/assets, working capital/assets, total assets, and equity/(equity+debt). For bank ratings, additional controls include sector fixed effects, current account balance, GDP growth volatility, equity/assets, loan growth, operation expenses/assets, net interest margin, deposits/assets, and total assets. For sovereign ratings, additional controls include country dummies, external balance, fiscal balance, default history, and external debt. All regressions were estimated by panel OLS, using annual data over 1995–2005. Robust standard errors, clustered by country-year in the corporate and bank rating regressions, are in parentheses. ***, **, and * denote statistical significance at the 1, 5, and 10 percent level, respectively.

Robustness: The regressions in the table are estimated with contemporaneous control variables (except for the sovereign ratings regressions); results are broadly similar when controls are lagged one period. The results also hold when the sample is restricted to industrial or emerging markets, and, in the corporate ratings regressions, when firms in the tradable and nontradable sectors are considered separately.

V STRUCTURAL REFORMS AND ECONOMIC GROWTH

Table 5.12. Effects of Trade Reforms on Financial Depth

Dependent Variable: Change in Log of Private Credit to GDP (t)	(1)	(2)
Change in index of average tariff ($t-1$)	−0.087 (0.077)	
Change in index of current account restrictions ($t-1$)		0.154** (0.072)
Change in domestic financial sector liberalization ($t-1$)	0.211*** (0.061)	0.172*** (0.056)
Change in external capital account liberalization ($t-1$)	0.037* (0.021)	0.020 (0.021)
Change in log of private credit to GDP ($t-1$)	0.460*** (0.044)	0.470*** (0.032)
Observations	1,671	1,622
R-squared	0.36	0.37

Sources: IMF staff estimates based on Abiad, Detragiache, and Tressel (2008); IMF, *International Financial Statistics*; and World Bank, *World Development Indicators*.

Notes: The table shows regressions of the change in financial depth, measured as the change in the private credit to GDP ratio, on lagged changes in financial, trade, and external capital account liberalization indices. All specifications were estimated by panel OLS with year fixed effects, using annual data over 1975–2006. Robust standard errors in parentheses. ***, **, and * denote statistical significance at the 1, 5, and 10 percent level, respectively.

Robustness: Results are robust to the inclusion of the rate of inflation, GDP per capita, real GDP growth, and a dummy for hyperinflation as control variables. The effect of reforms is also robust when estimated on the subsample of developing countries.

Table 5.13. Foreign Direct Investment Inflows and Real Sector Reforms

Dependent Variable: Log FDI/GDP (t)	Trade Liberalization (Tariff) (1)	Trade Liberalization (Current Account) (2)	Agricultural Liberalization (3)	Telecommunications and Electricity Liberalization (4)
Liberalization index ($t-1$)	0.406 (0.357)	0.094 (0.411)	0.231 (0.369)	0.636** (0.295)
Observations	2,418	1,550	1,810	1,956
Number of countries	119	59	92	94
Adjusted R-squared	0.62	0.61	0.59	0.58

Sources: IMF staff estimates based on IMF, *International Financial Statistics*; Penn World Tables version 6.2; and World Bank, *World Development Indicators*.

Notes: The table shows regressions of inward FDI, measured as the log of FDI to GDP, on real sector liberalization indices. Each regression includes controls for the growth of real per capita GDP, the level of development (proxied by the lagged level of real GDP per capita), market size (proxied by the lagged level of real GDP), and inflation. All regressions were estimated by panel OLS and include country and year fixed effects, using annual data over 1961–2006. Robust standard errors, clustered at the country-year level, are in parentheses. ***, **, and * denote statistical significance at the 1, 5, and 10 percent level, respectively.

VI Sequencing Real and Financial Sector Reforms

The analysis so far has considered the impact of individual reforms, rather than packages of multiple reforms, on economic growth. In practice, policymakers will wish to act on the basis of a reform strategy that takes into account sequencing issues as well as possible complementarities among reforms on expected growth outcomes. While political constraints may often be paramount in determining what can be achieved and when, policymakers will opt for reform strategies that are likely to have the most favorable impact on economic welfare or growth subject to the other constraints. Although there is a large literature on the design and sequencing of reform packages, including, for example, whether "big bang" or piecemeal approaches to reform yield greater economic returns, the *empirical* evidence on the growth benefits of alternative sequencing strategies, and indeed, as a prior matter, the "stylized facts" of reform sequencing strategies—what countries have actually pursued in practice—are relatively scarce.[14] This section examines the cross-country evidence on sequencing strategies and their growth effects, linking it where appropriate to the existing theoretical/normative work on these issues, which holds that

- *International trade should be liberalized before the external capital account.* McKinnon (1973) argued that liberalizing capital *inflows* before trade was likely to amplify the distortions caused by tariffs and reduce the competitiveness of domestic firms through real appreciation. Liberalizing capital *outflows* before trade would be equally undesirable if trade restrictions misallocate resources and depress domestic returns to the point that domestic capital would leave the economy. For both reasons, McKinnon, and others following him, have advocated a "trade reform first" strategy, contending that the growth benefits of reform would be higher under such a strategy than under alternative sequencing strategies.

- *The domestic financial sector should be liberalized before the external capital account.* In the presence of regulated interest rates and other financial system distortions, capital mobility is likely to be destabilizing: capital *inflows* could lead to overborrowing in foreign currency, which a dysfunctional domestic financial sector would misallocate, and capital *outflows* could erode the domestic deposit base (McKinnon, 1973). There is some evidence that capital account liberalization may increase volatility and crisis risk in the absence of a sufficiently reformed domestic financial sector (Dell'Ariccia and others, 2008). If such volatility leads to an inefficient allocation of resources, growth should be higher when the domestic financial sector is reformed before the external capital account than under the reverse sequencing strategy.

- *Trade should be liberalized before the domestic financial sector.* Opening the economy to international trade first has been argued to make subsequent reform of the domestic financial sector more likely because greater competition in product markets (through trade) is likely to weaken the influence of monopolistic incumbents who may oppose financial development (Rajan and Zingales, 2003). While this argument may explain why trade reform is more likely to precede domestic financial sector reform than vice versa, it does not necessarily imply that growth should be higher under the first sequence than the second.

To what extent do countries actually follow the sequencing prescriptions advocated in the normative literature? Table 6.1 presents evidence on actual sequencing practices, by testing whether some reform indicators are leading indicators of—that is, generally precede—changes in other reform indicators. Specifically, five-year changes in the indicators of domestic financial sector liberalization (column 1), external capital account liberalization (column 2), and the tariff-based trade liberalization index (column 3) are regressed on five-year lags of all other reform indicators, controlling for a variety of other determinants of liberalization. The results suggest that trade liberalization does indeed help to predict future reform of both the domestic financial sector

---

[14]Bhattacharya (1997) provides a review of the theoretical literature. Previous empirical work has focused on the sequencing of product and labor market reforms for OECD countries (Fiori and others, 2007), but has generally ignored the broader sequencing issues among the different sectors covered in this paper. A related issue, well outside the remit of this paper, concerns the appropriate sequencing between macroeconomic stabilization and structural reforms; see Zalduendo (2005) for an analysis.

VI SEQUENCING REAL AND FINANCIAL SECTOR REFORMS

Table 6.1. Sequencing of Structural Reforms

Dependent Variable: Reform Index (t) – Reform Index (t–5)	Domestic Financial Sector Liberalization (1)	External Capital Account Liberalization (2)	Trade Liberalization (Tariff) (3)
Trade liberalization (tariff) (t–5)	0.107***	0.235**	–0.578***
	(0.04)	(0.10)	(0.08)
Domestic financial sector liberalization (t–5)	–0.694***	0.189	–0.030
	(0.07)	(0.13)	(0.06)
External capital account liberalization (t–5)	–0.031	–0.839***	0.034
	(0.03)	(0.08)	(0.03)
Observations	353	353	352
Number of countries	74	74	74
Adjusted R-squared	0.44	0.43	0.32

Source: IMF staff estimates.

Notes: The table shows regressions of five-year changes in the indicators of domestic financial sector liberalization (column 1), external capital account liberalization (column 2), and trade (tariff) liberalization (column 3) on five-year lags of all other liberalization indices. Explanatory variables include indices of liberalization in agriculture and in the telecommunications and electricity industries, the own lagged levels of the index considered, country and year fixed effects, and a measure of the level of liberalization in neighboring countries. All specifications were estimated by panel OLS on nonoverlapping five-year intervals over the period 1975–2000. Robust standard errors are reported in parentheses. ***, **, and * denote statistical significance at 1, 5, and 10 percent level, respectively.

Robustness: The trade liberalization index based on current account restrictions has leading indicator properties similar to those of the reported tariff-based index. Broadly similar results are obtained including, as additional controls, five-year lags of GDP per capita, a terms of trade index, and an indicator variable for democratic regimes.

and the external capital account (first row), while it is not itself predicted by either of the other reforms (last column), consistent with the "trade-first" strategy advocated in the normative literature. The data, however, do not speak loudly on whether domestic financial sector liberalization leads or lags external capital account liberalization. The estimated coefficient on domestic financial sector liberalization in the external capital account reform regression (second column/second row) is borderline significant, providing only weak evidence that countries tend to reform the domestic financial sector before opening up to foreign capital.

What about the growth effects of alternative sequencing strategies? Figure 6.1 illustrates the evolution of the indices of domestic financial sector and external capital account liberalization, as well as the tariff-based index of trade liberalization, before and after growth breaks. Overall, the trade-first sequence seems to be associated with growth upbreaks, while a trade-last sequence seems to characterize growth downbreaks. Specifically:

- In the run-up to growth upbreaks, economies have generally already introduced trade reforms, with the trade liberalization index above the country average (top panel of Figure 6.1). In contrast, in the run-up to downbreaks, economies have yet to open to trade (bottom panel). This suggests that a liberal trade regime is involved both in igniting growth and in sustaining it—the latter result is also strongly supported by the analysis of growth duration in Berg, Ostry, and Zettelmeyer (2008).

- During acceleration episodes, the top panel of Figure 6.1 shows that the index of domestic financial sector liberalization and that of external capital account liberalization are on a rising trend three to four years before the upbreak. Thus, an open trade regime, together with an increasingly liberalized domestic financial sector and external capital account, appear to be an integral part of acceleration episodes, with the latter two reforms mostly progressing together. In contrast, a relatively open external capital account, combined with a relatively closed trade account and domestic financial sector reforms about equal to country averages, seems to be a common feature of growth decelerations.

Econometric evidence corroborates the main results from Figure 6.1 regarding the growth effects of different reform sequencing strategies. Table 6.2 presents results on the effects of alternative pairwise sequencing strategies, controlling for standard growth determinants and the direct effects of reforms.[15] The positive and statisti-

---

[15]Specifically, the regressions control for several standard variables, such as per capita GDP, terms of trade shocks, tertiary edu-

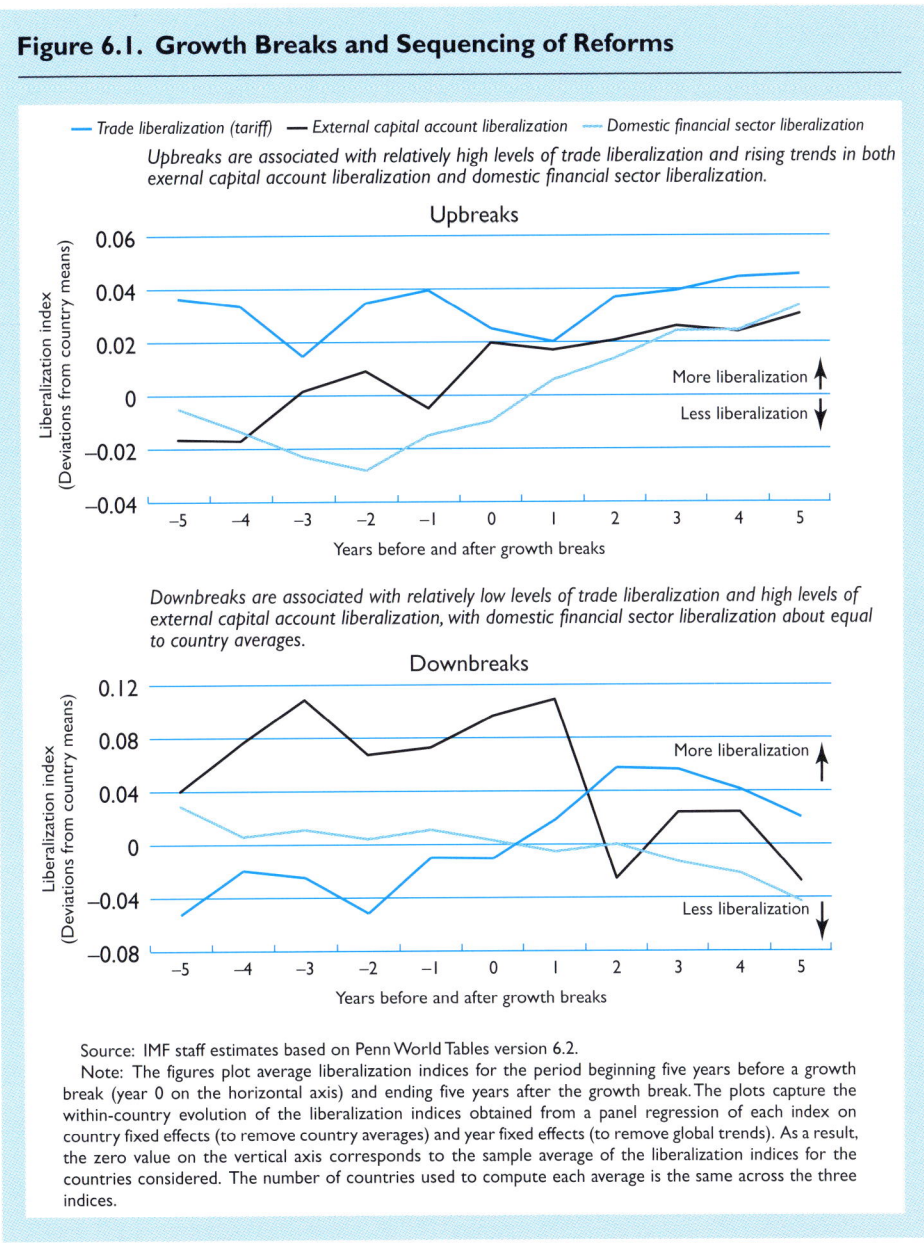

Figure 6.1. Growth Breaks and Sequencing of Reforms

— Trade liberalization (tariff) — External capital account liberalization — Domestic financial sector liberalization

Upbreaks are associated with relatively high levels of trade liberalization and rising trends in both external capital account liberalization and domestic financial sector liberalization.

Downbreaks are associated with relatively low levels of trade liberalization and high levels of external capital account liberalization, with domestic financial sector liberalization about equal to country averages.

Source: IMF staff estimates based on Penn World Tables version 6.2.
Note: The figures plot average liberalization indices for the period beginning five years before a growth break (year 0 on the horizontal axis) and ending five years after the growth break. The plots capture the within-country evolution of the liberalization indices obtained from a panel regression of each index on country fixed effects (to remove country averages) and year fixed effects (to remove global trends). As a result, the zero value on the vertical axis corresponds to the sample average of the liberalization indices for the countries considered. The number of countries used to compute each average is the same across the three indices.

cally significant coefficient on the trade-before-external-capital-account liberalization sequencing term (first row/second column) indicates that liberalizing trade before the capital account yields a more favorable growth outcome

cation, political institutions, and country and time dummies. In addition, the regressions estimate the direct growth effects of reforms X and Y, possible complementarities between reforms through an interaction term $X*Y$, and a sequencing effect represented by a second interaction term $X*Y*(\%X-\%Y)$, where $\%X$ denotes the percentile of a country's level of reform X in a given year in the regression sample.

The sequencing term reflects the extent to which more progress in one reform (i.e., a higher percentile) than in the other reform affects the complementarity of two reforms. Thus, a positive coefficient implies that more reform progress on X than Y is preferable to the reverse. The interaction between the product of the indices and their difference helps distinguish between the case in which the same product of the indices is achieved with a high value of the first liberalization index and a low value of the second (sequencing from the first to the second reform), vice versa (sequencing from the second to the first reform), or similar values of both indices (no sequencing). In fact, as Table 6.1 shows, the coefficient on the complementarity term is typically negative, that is, reforms typically are partial substitutes in their effects on growth. A positive coefficient on the sequencing term then implies that proper sequencing reduces the substitution effect and raises the total growth benefits of reform.

VI SEQUENCING REAL AND FINANCIAL SECTOR REFORMS

Table 6.2. Growth Effects of Alternative Reform Sequencing Strategies

Dependent Variable: Annual Per Capita GDP Growth (t)	Trade Liberalization (Tariff) Versus Domestic Financial Sector Liberalization (1)	Trade Liberalization (Tariff) Versus External Capital Account Liberalization (2)	Domestic Financial Sector Liberalization Versus External Capital Account Liberalization (3)
Reform sequence (first reform before second) ($t-1$)	0.03 (0.019)	0.043** (0.018)	0.052 (0.046)
Direct effect (first reform) ($t-1$)	0.019* (0.010)	0.026** (0.011)	0.071*** (0.016)
Direct effect (second reform) ($t-1$)	0.062*** (0.023)	0.058*** (0.017)	0.034** (0.014)
Reform complementarity ($t-1$)	−0.018 (0.024)	−0.051** (0.020)	−0.054** (0.021)
Observations	1,991	1,991	2,114
Number of countries	88	88	88
Adjusted R-squared	0.06	0.06	0.08

Sources: IMF staff estimates based on IMF, *International Financial Statistics*; Penn World Tables version 6.2; and World Bank, *World Development Indicators*.

Notes: This table shows regressions of annual per capita GDP growth on various (pairwise) combinations of reform. The effects of reforms are disaggregated into a direct effect; a reform complementarity effect captured by a multiplicative interaction of the two liberalization indices; and a sequencing effect. The latter is constructed by first calculating, for each reform, the percentile of a country's liberalization index in a given year (based on the respective regression sample), and then interacting the difference in the percentiles with the complementarity term. The sequencing term thus captures the difference between the extent of liberalization across the two sectors. Control variables include: the level of GDP per capita (in logs), the level of terms of trade, an indicator variable for democratic regimes, the level of tertiary education, all lagged one year. All regressions were estimated by panel OLS including country and time fixed effects. Robust standard errors are provided in parentheses. ***, **, and * denote statistical significance at the 1, 5, and 10 percent level, respectively.

Robustness: Results are robust to measuring the reform sequence term using actual liberalization indices rather than their percentiles.

Table 6.3. Cumulative Growth Effects of Alternative Reform Sequences: A Numerical Example
(In percent)

	Reform Sequence of Trade Versus External Capital Account		
	Simultaneous ("big bang")	Trade openness (tariff) before external capital account openness	External capital account openness before trade openness (tariff)
Sequencing	0.0	7.5	−11.7
Direct	43.6	27.3	57.9
Interaction	−31.5	−20.0	−34.8
Total	12.1	14.8	11.4

Source: IMF staff estimates.

Notes: The example is based on the regression specification in column 2 of Table 5.13; it assumes a reform package over 15 years, with both trade and external capital account openness initially at the 25th percentile and eventually reaching the 75th percentile. In column 2, starting in the second year, trade openness is assumed to gradually increase until the 75th percentile is reached in the 8th year, remaining constant from then onwards, while external capital account liberalization starts in the 9th year, reaching the 75th percentile in the 15th year; column 3 is the reverse of column 2. In column 1 ("big bang"), both trade and the external capital account are liberalized simultaneously; to maintain broadly the same total number of reform years as in columns 2 and 3, the start of reform in column 1 is delayed until the 5th year, thus reaching the 75th percentile in the 11th year. The growth numbers are cumulative increases in output over 15 years, in excess of those that would have occurred in the absence of reform (i.e., if both indices had remained at their respective 25th percentile over the entire 15-year period).

than the reverse sequence.[16] By contrast, no clear ranking—in terms of growth outcomes—emerges between domestic financial sector liberalization and the opening of the external capital account (column 3), or between trade and domestic financial sector liberalization (the sequence with trade first is only borderline significant in column 1).

The benefits from appropriate reform sequencing can be economically significant. Based on the regression results in Table 6.2, column 2 (trade versus external capital account liberalization), Table 6.3 provides numerical examples of the growth effects of alternative reform sequencing strategies over a 15-year horizon. To keep alternative sequencing strategies comparable, growth paths were calculated for three scenarios. In each scenario, both trade and capital account indices are initially at the 25th percentile of their respective sample distribution. In the simultaneous reform ("big bang") scenario, starting in the 5th year, both the trade and capital account indices increase linearly until they reach their respective 75th percentiles in the 11th year. In the "preferred sequencing" (trade before capital account liberalization) scenario, trade moves up to the 75th percentile during years two through eight, while capital account liberalization moves from the 25th to the 75th percentile during years 9 through 15. Finally, in the trade-after-capital-account-liberalization scenario, the reform sequence is the reverse of the second scenario.

The trade-before-capital-account reform sequence has by far the most favorable impact on per capita income levels, raising per capita GDP growth by an annual 1.4 percent during the 15-year horizon compared to a no-reform scenario (in which both reform indicators remain at their 25th percentiles), and, notably, by almost a ¼ percentage point relative to the "big bang" approach where reforms are pursued simultaneously. By contrast, the reverse sequence of capital account liberalization, while still better than no reform, performs worse than the simultaneous reform case, and yields annual growth about ⅓ percentage point lower than the trade-first sequence. Thus, when possible, implementing reforms in the correct order is likely to yield substantial growth benefits.

---

[16]To make the level of liberalization comparable across sectors, the indices were transformed into percentiles of the distribution of each index. Estimating the regressions with the raw indices yields similar results.

VII Financial Sector Reforms and Resilience

How do structural reforms and, in particular, financial sector reforms affect macroeconomic volatility and resilience? In principle, financial reforms should help buffer economies against the effects of adverse shocks, facilitate adjustment to such shocks, and thereby foster greater risk sharing at the economy-wide level. Intuitively, a financial sector that efficiently allocates credit can provide firms with liquidity and reduce inefficient closures when shocks occur (Bernanke and Gertler, 1989; and Kiyotaki and Moore, 1997). To address what is in essence an empirical issue, Figure 7.1 shows how output volatility (top panel) and the frequency of "sudden stops" (bottom panel) vary with the level of financial liberalization.[17] The results suggest that countries with a relatively liberalized domestic financial sector seem to enjoy lower macroeconomic volatility and experience a lower incidence of sudden stops, while the association between external capital account liberalization and macroeconomic volatility/crisis propensity appears to be weak. Of course, just as the growth effects of structural reforms depend critically on the sequencing strategy pursued, so too the above volatility/crisis risk results also reflect reform sequencing. Specifically, as shown in Table 7.1, volatility and crisis risk are low when the domestic financial sector and the external capital account are both relatively liberalized, while volatility and crisis risk are high when the external capital account is relatively liberalized but domestic financial sector liberalization is low. The results in Figure 7.1 thus would seem to aggregate very different macro-volatility profiles from domestic financial reform and external capital account liberalization, which depend critically on the sequencing strategy pursued.

Figure 7.2 comes to the volatility issue from a different angle, by examining whether liberalization of the domestic financial sector helps to buffer economies against terms of trade shocks, a key source of volatility in low- and middle-income countries. Results suggest that, in countries with more liberalized domestic financial sectors, growth rebounds faster after a negative terms of trade shock (Figure 7.2). Results reported in Ramcharan (forthcoming) suggest that the magnitude of the benefit from reform is substantial: after a decline in the terms of trade of 10 percentage points, a one standard deviation difference in the domestic financial sector liberalization index is associated with a cumulative income per capita growth that is 1.3 percentage points higher over a five-year period. The enhanced resilience provided by domestic financial sector liberalization extends to a variety of other real shocks—such as windstorms, floods, and earthquakes (Ramcharan, 2007)—where greater credit availability provides a key channel buffering the aggregate output effects from such shocks.

Sectoral evidence also shows that those manufacturing sectors more exposed to terms of trade shocks—specifically, those that use relatively more imported intermediate inputs in production—experience a growth deceleration, following a negative terms of trade shock, which is relatively smaller in countries with more liberalized domestic financial systems. Specifically, Table 7.2 illustrates regressions of the change in sectoral output growth in the three years following a negative terms of trade shock relative to the three years preceding the shock. An episode of a negative terms of trade shock is defined as a year during which the terms of trade deteriorates by more than 10 percent relative to the previous years (considering alternative thresholds does not affect the main result). During such episodes, annual manufacturing output growth on average declines by 5 percentage points over a three year period.

The results imply that domestic financial liberalization has an economically significant impact on relative output growth following a negative terms of trade shock. For instance, a sector importing about 30 percent of its inputs will experience an output growth deceleration (relative to the output growth deceleration of a sector that imports 20 percent of its inputs) that is about 0.5 percentage point smaller in a country with a banking sector reform index that is one standard deviation higher. These results confirm the role of financial development in dampening the adverse effects of financial fragility (Raddatz, 2006). This evidence is consistent with existing theories emphasizing the role

---

[17]In principle, while there may be a connection between real sector reforms and output volatility, the data do not speak loudly on such a linkage, hence the focus in this section on the association between financial sector liberalization and resilience to shocks.

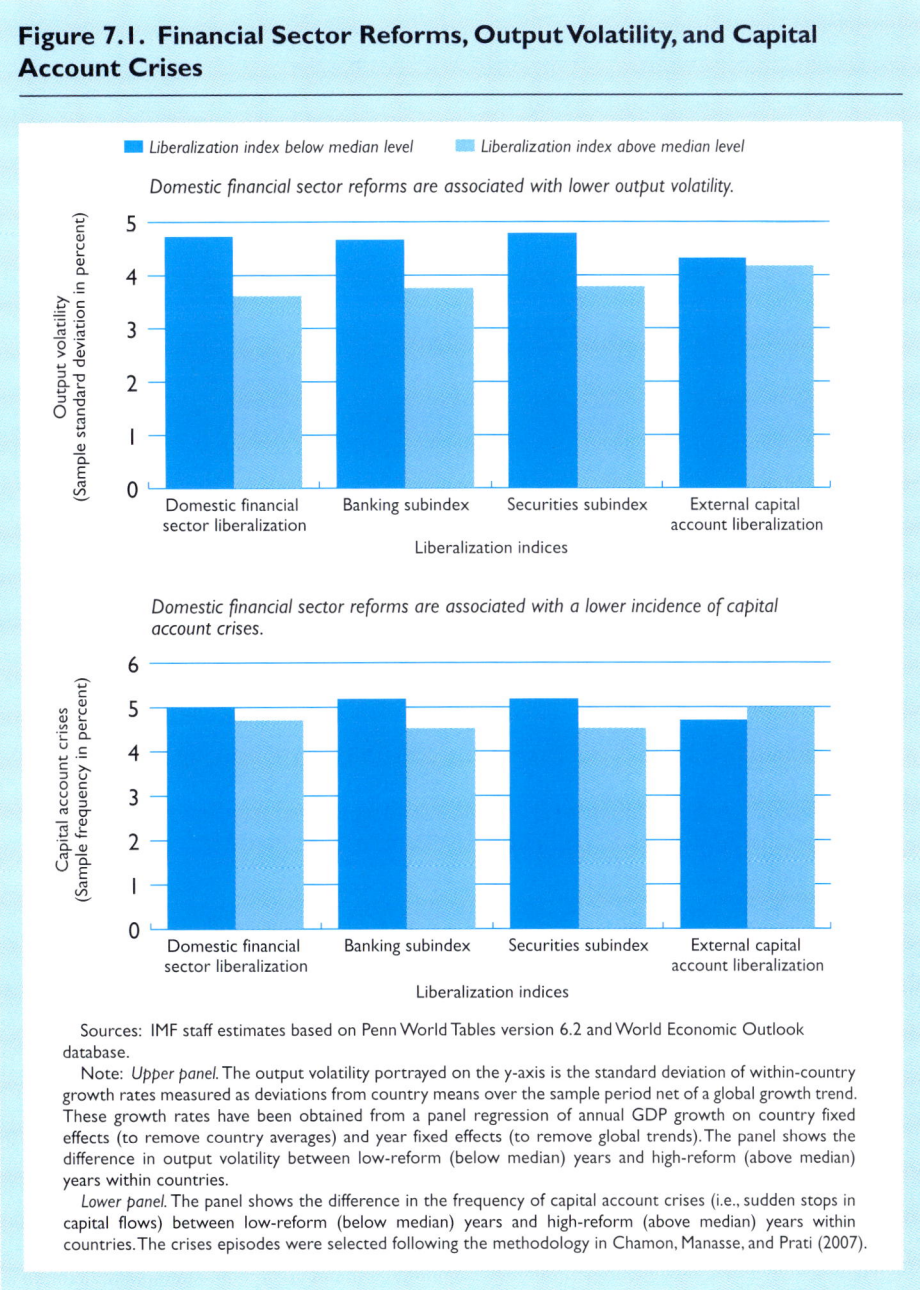

Figure 7.1. Financial Sector Reforms, Output Volatility, and Capital Account Crises

Sources: IMF staff estimates based on Penn World Tables version 6.2 and World Economic Outlook database.

Note: *Upper panel.* The output volatility portrayed on the y-axis is the standard deviation of within-country growth rates measured as deviations from country means over the sample period net of a global growth trend. These growth rates have been obtained from a panel regression of annual GDP growth on country fixed effects (to remove country averages) and year fixed effects (to remove global trends). The panel shows the difference in output volatility between low-reform (below median) years and high-reform (above median) years within countries.

Lower panel. The panel shows the difference in the frequency of capital account crises (i.e., sudden stops in capital flows) between low-reform (below median) years and high-reform (above median) years within countries. The crises episodes were selected following the methodology in Chamon, Manasse, and Prati (2007).

of financial frictions in propagating economic fluctuations (Bernanke and Gertler, 1989; Holmstrom and Tirole, 1997; and Aghion and others, 2005), as well as with theories that describe the mechanisms through which well-functioning financial systems have a positive impact on the development process (Banerjee and Newman, 1991; and Greenwood and Jovanovic, 1990).

Domestic financial sector liberalization also enhances the resilience of the economy to financial shocks. Specifically, the market structure of the banking system is often a key component of financial sector reforms. A perennial question in finance is whether policies that promote competition in the banking sector might also influence the resilience of the financial system to liquidity shocks (Carletti and Hartmann, 2002). The evidence suggests that, after a 1 percentage point increase in foreign interest rates, economies that score at the 75th percentile on the banking sector competi-

VII FINANCIAL SECTOR REFORMS AND RESILIENCE

Table 7.1. Financial Sector Reforms, Output Volatility, and Capital Account Crises

	External Capital Account Liberalization		
	High	Intermediate	Low
	Output volatility *(Percentage points)*		
Domestic financial sector liberalization			
High	2.8	4.6	3.1
Intermediate	3.6	5.0	4.2
Low	8.1	6.4	4.6
	Frequency of sudden stops *(Percentage points, annual basis)*		
Domestic financial sector liberalization			
High	4.0	3.9	5.6
Intermediate	6.2	3.8	5.5
Low	6.7	6.5	4.7

Source: IMF staff calculations.

Notes: The terms "high," "intermediate," and "low" indicate that the value of the relevant index falls into, respectively, the top 25 percent, the intermediate 50 percent, and the bottom 25 percent of the overall distribution. In the top panel, the values in each cell indicate the average standard deviation of annual GDP growth under different degrees of external capital account and domestic financial sector liberalization, controlling for country and year fixed effects. In the bottom panel, the values in each cell indicate the sample frequency of sudden stops (see Chamon, Manasse, and Prati (2007) for the definition).

tion subindex enjoy a cumulative income per capita growth, over a five-year period, that is 3 percentage points higher than economies at the median level of banking competition (Ramcharan, forthcoming). This buffering role of banking sector competition is likely to reflect risk diversification benefits from fewer restrictions on the number and geographical location of bank branches (see Box 7.1).

Figure 7.2. Terms of Trade Shocks and the Financial Sector

With a more liberalized domestic financial system, adverse terms of trade shocks are less costly in terms of forgone output.

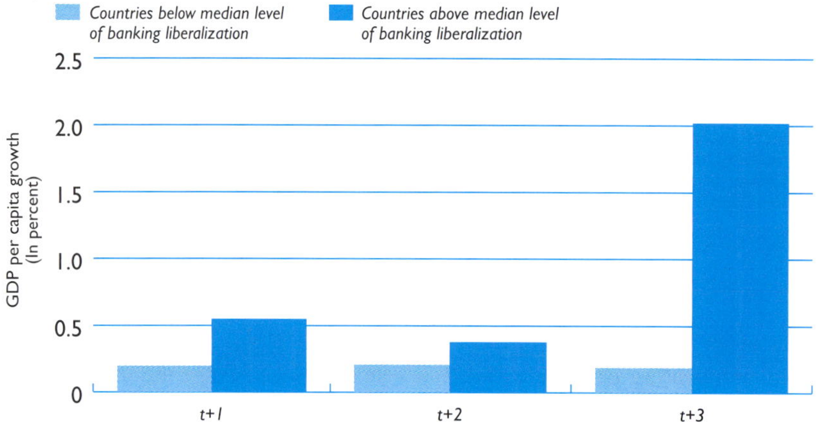

Source: IMF staff calculations.

Note: This figure plots median growth rates in the three years following a negative terms of trade shock. A negative terms of trade shock for each country is defined as a decline of one or more standard deviations in the growth in the terms of trade. The figure shows separately the growth rates for country-year pairs above and below the median level of banking sector liberalization. These growth rates have been obtained from a panel regression of annual GDP growth on country fixed effects (to remove country averages) and year fixed effects (to remove global trends).

Table 7.2. Financial Sector Reforms and Resilience to Terms of Trade Shocks

Dependent Variable: Change in Sectoral Output Growth in the Three Years Following a Terms of Trade Shock	(1)	(2)	(3)
Domestic financial liberalization index interacted with a measure of imported input intensity (t–3)	0.181*** (0.056)	0.229*** (0.052)	0.183*** (0.059)
Private credit/GDP interacted with a measure of imported input intensity (t–3)		–0.068 (0.044)	
Growth rate of terms of trade interacted with a measure of imported input intensity (t)			–0.185 (0.56)
Log output share (t–3)	–0.006 (0.009)	–0.006 (0.009)	–0.006 (0.009)
Observations	995	978	995
R-squared	0.13	0.14	0.13

Sources: IMF staff estimates based on the GTAP database, and Abiad, Detragiache, and Tressel (2008); United Nations Industrial Development Organization, 2006 Industrial Statistics Database; and World Bank, *World Development Indicators*.

Notes: The table shows regressions of the change in sectoral output growth of manufacturing industries in the three years following a terms of trade shock on the domestic financial sector liberalization index interacted with a measure of imported input intensity and a number of controls. The interaction term captures the differential effect of domestic financial sector liberalization on the resilience of industries that are relatively more exposed to shocks. Terms of trade shock episodes are defined as years with a 10 percentage point or greater annual drop in the terms of trade. The first column shows the baseline regression, the second and third columns show that results are robust when controlling for interactions of the measure of imported input intensity with, respectively, the private credit-to-GDP ratio and the intensity of the terms of trade shock. All regressions were estimated using OLS and include country, industry, and year dummies. Robust standard errors, clustered at the country-year level, are in parentheses. ***, **, and * denote statistical significance at the 1, 5, and 10 percent level, respectively.

Robustness: Robustness checks included controlling for an interaction term between the measure of imported input intensity and (1) indicators of trade liberalization; (2) the overall level of development (real GDP per capita); (3) an indicator variable for the type of legal system (common law or civil law); (4) an indicator of contract enforcement; and (5) indicators of property rights. A complete set of results is reported in Tressel (2008).

VII FINANCIAL SECTOR REFORMS AND RESILIENCE

Box 7.1. Banking Sector Competition and Macroeconomic Stability

Do policies that promote competition in the banking sector compromise financial and macroeconomic stability (Carletti and Hartmann, 2002)? This question has taken on increased resonance with the recent banking crises in the United States, but has long featured in debates over banking competition and stability. After the severe banking crises of the 1930s in the United States, most states eventually restricted competition, barring the entry of banks chartered in other states in order to preserve stability. Modern debates, driven in part by periodic banking crises in emerging markets over the last two decades, also focus on the role of entry barriers and similar regulations in making the financial sector more resilient to external liquidity and other shocks (Kaminsky and Reinhart, 1999; and Mishkin, 2001).

In particular, allowing banks to earn monopoly rents can limit excessive risk taking, especially in response to the moral hazard related to deposit insurance and other public guarantees (Allen and Gale (2000)). Extending this intuition, Dell'Ariccia and Marquez (2006) model the idea that lending standards can decline as banks compete to gain market share during booms. The resulting expansion of credit to potentially low-quality borrowers can make the banking system more vulnerable to aggregate liquidity shocks. However, Boyd and De Nicolò (2005) argue that because monopolies charge higher interest rates on loans, borrowers are likely to adjust their investments by taking on more risk. As a result, interest rate increases and other aggregate shocks might lead to wider default among borrowers in monopolistic banking systems. Also, while regulatory entry barriers can increase the rents of incumbent banks, they limit the risk diversification opportunities of banks across space, potentially increasing the vulnerability of the financial system to liquidity shocks.

To explore the relationship between banking sector competition and the economy's resilience to liquidity shocks, we turn to external interest rate movements. These movements can affect the liquidity available to domestic banking systems, and often influence economic outcomes in developing countries (Di Giovanni and Shambaugh, 2008).[1] The evidence consistently suggests that the output cost of external interest rate movements are significantly greater in economies ranked as having more regulatory entry barriers in the banking sector. For two otherwise similar countries, a standard deviation increase in the base interest rate is associated with a 1 percentage point (or 0.25 standard deviations) decline in real per capita output growth for a country with regulations that restrict bank competition. In contrast, for a country classified as having few entry restrictions on banking, a similar increase in the base rate leaves real per capita output growth practically unchanged.

These results are mainly driven by open capital account economies, and bear upon the debate on the link between capital account openness and financial sector stability.[2] The pass-through of base rate movements onto the domestic financial system is typically larger in open capital account economies. These economies are also more susceptible to sharp reversals in capital flows when external rates change. In this subsample of countries, a one standard deviation positive interest rate shock is associated with a 2.2 percentage point decline in output growth for countries with regulations that restrict bank entry. There is a slight increase in output growth of about 0.12 percentage points in regulatory environments that favor banking competition. Moreover, when foreign rates increase, higher entry barriers in this subsample are also associated with a higher probability of banking crises, and greater rigidity in domestic deposit rates.[3]

Taken together, this evidence appears most consistent with those models that suggest that lower entry barriers and policies that promote banking competition might also enhance the resilience of the financial system to external liquidity and other shocks. The results also imply that, in the absence of these domestic financial sector policies, capital account openness might actually increase financial and economic instability.

---

[1] Neumeyer and Perri (2005) model the business cycle impact of foreign interest rates. In addition to Di Giovanni and Shambaugh (2008), see also Reinhart and Rogoff (2008) and Reinhart and Reinhart (2001) for evidence on the impact of economic outcomes in financial centers on periphery countries.
[2] See the recent survey in Kose and others (2006).
[3] Beck and others (2005) also find that competition-friendly regulatory environments are less prone to banking crises.

VIII Conclusions

Maintaining sound economic growth, together with broad financial stability, is a perennial challenge for policymakers in developed and developing countries alike, and understanding the role that structural reforms may play in meeting this challenge remains a central element of surveillance for all segments of the IMF's membership. This paper has sought to draw lessons from the cross-country experience on structural reform, so as to strengthen the underpinnings of IMF policy advice and surveillance across the membership.

Past analyses of structural reforms have mainly focused on industrial countries, for which indicators of structural reform liberalization are readily available, or on selected groups of countries or regions of the world. In contrast, the present study rests on a new dataset, which includes comparable indicators of structural reforms for 91 developing, emerging market, and advanced economies over the past three decades, as well as an extensive coverage of different economic sectors. The broad cross-country and cross-sectoral approach is essential for drawing policy lessons across different segments of the IMF's membership, and for addressing empirically issues related to policy sequencing.

With respect to the causes of structural reform, the empirical analysis suggests that the quality of broad institutions initially spurred liberalization among advanced economies, but that, as cross-country reform gaps—either with respect to reform "leaders" or with respect to reformist "neighbors"—emerged, a catch-up effect led to subsequent reform in developing countries. There is also evidence that IMF-supported programs and, for some sectors, economic crises have been a catalyst for reform.

Real and financial sector reforms have helped to boost economic growth in both developed and developing countries, with domestic financial sector liberalization, trade liberalization, and liberalization of the agricultural sector exerting particularly favorable effects. The channels through which growth effects operate include greater availability of credit and FDI inflows; and improvements in allocative efficiency, which have acted to boost growth particularly in firms and sectors heavily dependent on imported intermediate inputs and external sources of financing. The implementation of structural reforms has also tended to enhance the assessment of the future profitability and solvency of domestic firms, as reflected in credit ratings, with a corresponding reduction in borrowing costs for domestic firms and banks following liberalization.

The nature of the reform sequencing strategy pursued affects the size of the ensuing growth benefits. The cross-country evidence strongly suggests that economies that liberalize trade before the external capital account grow more rapidly than those that follow the reverse sequence, and that a "trade-first" strategy yields better growth results than a "big bang" approach under which liberalization is pursued simultaneously across all sectors. While there is no evidence that the sequencing of domestic financial sector and external capital account liberalization has a significant impact on growth outcomes, the stability benefits—in terms of both macroeconomic volatility and crisis propensity—are more favorable when the domestic financial sector is liberalized before the external capital account.

Domestic financial sector reforms also enhance the way in which economies respond to various real and financial shocks, as financial reforms reduce the output costs from adverse terms of trade and foreign interest rate shocks, with a variety of mechanisms—especially improvements in credit availability—playing a key role. The greater resilience to real shocks in economies with more liberalized financial sectors is evidence of how such reforms can strengthen economy-wide real-financial linkages.

The evidence presented in this paper—given its broad country, time, and sectoral coverage—should help to strengthen the cross-country perspective in bilateral surveillance on the role of structural policies in fostering sound medium-run growth-cum-stability in member countries. The results highlight the growth benefits of a reform strategy that relies on early trade liberalization and, in the context of a relatively open trade regime, accelerates the process of liberalizing both the domestic financial sector and the external capital account. The paper also highlights that, as long as the domestic financial sector is reformed before opening the capital account, structural reform can enhance growth opportunities without raising macroeconomic volatility or crisis risks. Appropriately sequenced structural reforms, thus, seem to improve the growth-volatility frontier for the economy, rather than simply engendering a move along the existing frontier.

Appendix   Data, Sources, and Methods

Table A1. List of Economies in the Sample

Low Income	Middle Income	High Income
Bangladesh	Albania	Australia
Burkina Faso	Algeria	Austria
Côte d'Ivoire	Argentina	Belgium
Ethiopia	Azerbaijan	Canada
Ghana	Belarus	Czech Republic
India	Bolivia	Denmark
Kenya	Brazil	Estonia
Madagascar	Bulgaria	Finland
Mozambique	Cameroon	France
Nepal	Chile	Germany
Nigeria	China	Greece
Pakistan	Colombia	Hong Kong SAR
Senegal	Costa Rica	Ireland
Tanzania	Dominican Republic	Israel
Uganda	Ecuador	Italy
Uzbekistan	Egypt	Japan
Vietnam	El Salvador	Korea
Zimbabwe	Georgia	Netherlands
	Guatemala	New Zealand
	Hungary	Norway
	Indonesia	Portugal
	Jamaica	Singapore
	Jordan	Spain
	Kazakhstan	Sweden
	Latvia	Switzerland
	Lithuania	Taiwan Province of China
	Malaysia	United Kingdom
	Mexico	United States
	Morocco	
	Nicaragua	
	Paraguay	
	Peru	
	Philippines	
	Poland	
	Romania	
	Russia	
	South Africa	
	Sri Lanka	
	Thailand	
	Tunisia	
	Turkey	
	Ukraine	
	Uruguay	
	Venezuela, Rep. Bolivariana	

Source: World Bank.

Appendix

Table A2. Description of Reform Indices

Reform Indices	Description	Source	Start year	End year	Coverage Minimum number of countries in any year	Coverage Maximum number of countries in any year
Financial sector						
Domestic financial sector liberalization	The index of domestic financial liberalization is an average of six subindices. Five of them relate to banking: (1) interest rate controls, such as floors or ceilings; (2) credit controls, such as directed credit and subsidized lending; (3) competition restrictions, such as limits on branches and entry barriers in the banking sector, including licensing requirements or limits on foreign banks; (4) the degree of state ownership; and (5) the quality of banking supervision and regulation, including power of independence of bank supervisors, adoption of Basel capital standards, and a framework for bank inspections. The sixth subindex relates to securities markets and covers policies to develop domestic bond and equity markets, including (1) the creation of basic frameworks such as the auctioning of treasury bills or the establishment of a security commission; (2) policies to further establish securities markets such as tax exemptions, introduction of medium- and long-term government bonds to establish a benchmark for the yield curve, or the introduction of a primary dealer system; (3) policies to develop derivative markets or to create an institutional investor's base; and (4) policies to permit access to the domestic stock market by nonresidents. The subindices are aggregated with equal weights. Each subindex is coded from zero (fully repressed) to three (fully liberalized).	Abiad, Detragiache, and Tressel (2008), following the methodology in Abiad and Mody (2005), based on various IMF reports and working papers, central bank websites, and others.	1973	2005	72	91
External capital account liberalization: aggregate	Qualitative indicators of restrictions on financial credits and personal capital transactions of residents and financial credits to nonresidents, as well as the use of multiple exchange rates. Index coded from zero (fully repressed) to three (fully liberalized).	Abiad, Detragiache, and Tressel (2008), following the methodology in Abiad and Mody (2005), based on various IMF reports and working papers, central bank websites, and others.	1973	2005	72	91
External capital account liberalization: residents versus nonresidents	Indicators measuring the intensity of legal restrictions on residents' and nonresidents' ability to move capital into and out of a country. Index originally coded from zero (fully repressed) to 50 (fully liberalized).	Based on the methodology in Quinn (1997) and Quinn and Toyoda (2008), drawing on information contained in the IMF's *Annual Report on Exchange Arrangements and Exchange Restrictions* (AREAER).	1960	2005	50	65

APPENDIX

Table A2 (concluded)

Reform Indices	Description	Source	Start year	End year	Coverage Minimum number of countries in any year	Coverage Maximum number of countries in any year
Real sector						
Trade liberalization						
Tariff rates	Average tariff rates, with missing values extrapolated using implicit weighted tariff rates. Index normalized to be between zero and unity: zero means the tariff rates are 60 percent or higher, while unity means the tariff rates are zero.	Various sources, including IMF, World Bank, WTO, UN, and the academic literature (particularly Clemens and Williamson, 2004).	1960	2005	47	142
Current account restrictions	An indicator of how compliant a government is with its obligations under the IMF's Article VIII to free from government restriction the proceeds from international trade in goods and services. The index represents the sum of two subcomponents, dealing with restrictions on trade in visibles, as well as in invisibles (financial and other services). It distinguishes between restrictions on residents (receipts for exports) and on nonresidents (payments for imports). Although the index measures restrictions on the proceeds from transactions, rather than on the underlying transactions, many countries in practice use restrictions on trade proceeds as a type of trade restriction. The index is scored between zero and eight in half-integer units, with eight indicating full compliance.	Based on the methodology in Quinn (1997) and Quinn and Toyoda (2008), drawing on information contained in the IMF's AREAER.	1960	2005	50	65
Product markets						
Telecommunications and electricity industries	Simple average of the telecommunications and electricity markets subindices, which are constructed, in turn, from scores along three dimensions. For telecommunications, they capture: (1) the degree of competition in local services; (2) whether a regulator other than government has been established; and (3) the degree of liberalization of interconnection changes. Indices are coded with values ranging from zero (not liberalized) to two (completely liberalized). For electricity, they capture: (1) the degree of unbundling of generation, transmission, and distribution; (2) whether a regulator other than the government has been established; and (3) whether the wholesale market has been liberalized.	Based on various existing studies and datasets as well as national legislation and other official documents.	1960	2003	106	108
Agriculture	The index captures intervention in the market for the main agricultural export commodity in each country. As data limitations preclude coding separate dimensions of intervention, the index provides a summary measure. Each country-year pair can take four values: (1) zero (public monopoly or monopsony in production, transportation, or marketing, for example, export marketing boards); (2) one-third (administered prices); (3) two-thirds (public ownership of relevant producers or concession requirements); and (4) one (no public intervention).	Based on IMF commodities data, various existing studies and datasets, and national legislation and other official documents.	1960	2003	96	104

Appendix

Growth Spurts

The Underlying Methodology

This subsection discusses in greater depth the methodology used to identify growth spurts. This methodology is based on recent work by Antoshin, Berg, and Souto (2008) and Bai and Perron (1998 and 2003). Briefly, the Bai and Perron methodology first identifies a number of breaks in a time series, regardless of statistical significance. Once the breaks have been identified, it calculates a series of statistics to test for their statistical significance. However, the statistical significance tests proposed by Bai and Perron use asymptotic critical values, which are appropriate only when the sample is sufficiently large. As pointed out by Antoshin, Berg, and Souto, working with very small time series is inevitable in growth studies, because even for the most advanced countries reliable GDP data are scarce. These authors show via simulation exercises that statistics based on asymptotics can yield significant deviations in both size and power, especially when dealing with very small time series (with as low as 50 observations).

Antoshin, Berg, and Souto consequently propose modifying the Bai and Perron methodology to deal with small time series by using Monte Carlo simulations to determine sample-specific critical values under the null each time that the tests are run. Further, they provide practical suggestions on handling serial correlation, model misspecification, and the use of alternative test statistics for sequential testing. Finally, they show that, for most types of data generating processes in samples with as low as 50 observations, the proposed modifications represent a substantial improvement. For a more detailed discussion of the Bai-Perron and Antoshin-Berg-Souto methodologies, see Antoshin, Berg, and Souto (2008).

Discussion of Figures 5.2 and 5.4

Figures 5.2 and 5.4 plot the average level of the residuals from a panel regression of each index on country and year fixed effects for a period starting five years before the break (year zero on the horizontal axis) and ending five years after the break. All plotted averages are based on the set of countries for which the index is available three years before the break, so that each line shows how the average index has evolved around the break for the same group of countries. Given that the panel regression removes country- and year-specific averages of each index, a movement in the average residual from below to above the zero reference line prior to a growth upbreak (as in the case of the domestic financial liberalization index, top panel of Figure 5.2) indicates that the reform index has gone from below the country-average to above the country-average prior to the upbreak. The year-specific fixed effects effectively remove also the global trend in each index so that, in practice, the country-specific averages relative to which the plotted residuals are measured are trend-corrected. This means that a decline in the residual around growth downbreaks (as in the case of the current account and agriculture indices, middle and bottom panels of Figure 5.2) can indicate either reform reversals, or a lack of reform in a period where most other countries were reforming.

Specification of Growth Regressions

The results in Tables 5.1 and 5.6 are obtained by estimating simple OLS regressions based on the following specification:

$$\ln GDP_{i,t} - \ln GDP_{i,t-1} = a_0 + a_1 GDP_{i,t-1} + a_2 Reform_{i,t-1} + \eta_i + \delta_t + \varepsilon_{it}, \quad (1)$$

where the dependent variable is per capita GDP growth in country i at period t, regressed on lagged per capita GDP and each type of lagged real and financial reforms considered. η_i denotes the full set of country dummies, δ_t denotes the full set of time dummies, and ε_{it} captures all omitted effects. By including country fixed effects, we control for any country time-invariant characteristic (such as colonial legacies, legal origins, or ethnic fragmentation) that could affect both our measures of structural reforms and per capita income growth.

The results based on the Schumpeterian approach in Tables 5.2 and 5.8 are based on the following econometric specification:

$$\ln GDP_{i,t} - \ln GDP_{i,t-1} = a_0 + a_1 (GDP_{i,t-1}/GDP_{US,t-1}) + a_2 Reform_{i,t-1} + a_3 [Reform_{i,t-1} * (GDP_{i,t-1}/GDP_{US,t-1})] + \eta_i + \delta_t + \varepsilon_{it}, \quad (2)$$

where $GDP_{i,t-1}/GDP_{US,t-1}$ is the ratio of per capita GDP in country i to per capita GDP in the United States (an "income-gap" term that captures convergence), and $Reform_{i,t-1}*(GDP_{i,t-1}/GDP_{US,t-1})$ is an interaction between reform and income gap that captures the potential effect of reforms in closing the gap. If the interaction term is negative and significant, then the growth returns from reforming that sector will be larger the further a country is from the world output frontier.

References

Abiad, Abdul, Enrica Detragiache, and Thierry Tressel, 2008, "A New Database of Financial Reforms," IMF Working Paper 08/266 (Washington: International Monetary Fund).

Abiad, Abdul, and Ashoka Mody, 2005, "Financial Reform: What Shakes It? What Shapes It?" *American Economic Review*, Vol. 95 (March), No. 1, pp. 66–88.

Acemoglu, Daron, Philippe Aghion, and Fabrizio Zilibotti, 2006, "Distance to Frontier, Selection, and Economic Growth," *Journal of the European Economic Association*, Vol. 4, pp. 37–74.

Acemoglu, Daron, and Simon Johnson, 2005, "Unbundling Institutions," *Journal of Political Economy*, Vol. 113, No. 5, pp. 949–95.

Acemoglu, Daron, Simon Johnson, and James Robinson, 2001, "The Colonial Origins of Comparative Development: An Empirical Investigation," *American Economic Review*, Vol. 91 (December), pp. 1369–1401.

———, 2002, "Reversal of Fortune: Geography and Institutions in the Making of the Modern World Income Distribution," *Quarterly Journal of Economics*, Vol. 117, No. 3 (November), pp. 1231–94.

Acemoglu, Daron, Simon Johnson, James A. Robinson, and Yunyong Thaicharoen, 2003, "Institutional Causes, Macroeconomic Symptoms: Volatility, Crises and Growth," *Journal of Monetary Economics*, Vol. 50, No. 1 (January), pp. 49–123.

Aghion, Philippe, Alberto Alesina, and Francesco Trebbi, 2007, "Democracy, Technology and Growth," Harvard Institute of Economic Research Discussion Paper 2138 (Cambridge, Massachusetts: Harvard University).

Aghion, P., G-M. Angeletos, A. Banerjee, and K. Manova, 2005, "Volatility and Growth: Credit Constraints and Productivity-Enhancing Investment," NBER Working Paper No. 11349 (Cambridge, Massachusetts: National Bureau of Economic Research).

Aghion, Philippe, and Peter Howitt, 1992, "A Model of Growth Through Creative Destruction," *Econometrica*, Vol. 60, No. 2, pp. 323–51.

———, 2005, "Growth with Quality-Improving Innovations: An Integrated Framework," *Handbook of Economic Growth*, Vol. 1A, ed. by Philippe Aghion and Steven N. Durlauf (Amsterdam: North-Holland).

Allen, Franklin, and Douglas Gale, 2000, "Bubbles and Crises," *Economic Journal*, Vol. 110, No. 460 (January), pp. 236–55.

Amiti, Mary, and Jozef Konings, 2005, "Trade Liberalization, Intermediate Inputs, and Productivity: Evidence from Indonesia," IMF Working Paper 05/146 (Washington: International Monetary Fund).

Antoshin, Sergei, Andrew Berg, and Marcos Souto, 2008, "Testing for Structural Breaks in Small Samples," IMF Working Paper 08/75 (Washington: International Monetary Fund).

Bai, Jushan, and Pierre Perron, 1998, "Estimating and Testing Linear Models with Multiple Structural Changes," *Econometrica*, Vol. 66, No. 1, pp. 47–78.

———, 2003, "Critical Values for Multiple Structural Change Tests," *Econometrics Journal*, Vol. 6, No. 1, pp. 72–78.

Baltagi, Badi H., Panicos O. Demetriades, and Siong Hook Law, 2007, "Financial Development, Openness and Institutions: Evidence from Panel Data," Working Paper No. 0022, Birbeck College (London).

Banerjee, Abhijit, and Andrew Newman, 1991, "Risk-Bearing and the Theory of Income Distribution," *Review of Economic Studies*, Vol. 58, No. 2 (April), pp. 211–35.

Barro, Robert J., and Jong-Wha Lee, 2005, "IMF Programs: Who Is Chosen and What Are the Effects?" *Journal of Monetary Economics*, Vol. 52, No. 7, pp. 1245–69.

Beck, Thorsten, Ross Levine, and Norman Loayza, 2000, "Finance and the Sources of Growth," *Journal of Financial Economics*, Vol. 58, No. 1–2, pp. 261–300.

Beck, Thorsten, Asli Demirguc-Kunt, and Ross Levine, 2005, "Bank Concentration and Fragility: Impact and Mechanics," NBER Working Paper No. 11500 (Cambridge, Massachusetts: National Bureau of Economic Research).

Bekaert, Geert, Campbell R. Harvey, and Christian Lundblad, 2005, "Does Financial Liberalization Spur Growth?" *Journal of Financial Economics*, Vol. 77, No. 1, pp. 3–55.

Berg, Andrew, and Anne O. Krueger, 2003, "Trade, Growth, and Poverty: A Selective Survey," IMF Working Paper 03/30 (Washington: International Monetary Fund).

Berg, Andrew, Jonathan D. Ostry, and Jeromin Zettelmeyer, 2008, "What Makes Growth Sustained?" IMF Working Paper 08/59 (Washington: International Monetary Fund).

Bernanke, Ben, and Mark Gertler, 1989, "Agency Costs, Net Worth, and Business Fluctuations," *American Economic Review*, Vol. 79, No. 1 (March), pp. 14–31.

Bhattacharya, Rina, 1997, "Pace, Sequencing and Credibility of Structural Reforms," *World Development*, Vol. 25, No. 7, pp. 1045–61.

Binici, Mahir, Michael Hutchison, and Martin Schindler, 2009, "Controlling Capital? Legal Restrictions and the Asset Composition of International Financial Flows" (forthcoming IMF Working Paper; Washington: International Monetary Fund). Also forthcoming in *Journal of International Money and Finance*.

Blanchard, Olivier, and Francesco Giavazzi, 2003, "The Macroeconomic Effects of Regulation and Deregulation

References

in Goods and Labor Markets," *Quarterly Journal of Economics*, Vol. 118 (August), No. 3, pp. 879–907.

Boyd, John H., and Gianni De Nicolò, 2005, "The Theory of Bank Risk Taking and Competition Revisited," *Journal of Finance*, Vol. 60, No. 3, pp. 1329–43.

Boyd, John H., Ross Levine, and Bruce D. Smith, 2001, "The Impact of Inflation on Financial Sector Performance," *Journal of Monetary Economics*, Vol. 47, No. 2, pp. 221–48.

Braun, Matías, and Claudio Raddatz, 2008, "The Politics of Financial Development: Evidence from Trade Liberalization," *Journal of Finance*, Vol. 63, No. 3, pp. 1469–1508.

Broda, Christian, Joshua Greenfield, and David Weinstein, 2006, "From Groundnuts to Globalization: A Structural Estimate of Trade and Growth," NBER Working Paper No. 12512 (Cambridge, Massachusetts: National Bureau of Economic Research).

Carletti, Elena, and Philipp Hartmann, 2002, "Competition and Stability: What's Special About Banking?" Working Paper Series No. 146 (Frankfurt: European Central Bank).

Chamon, Marcos, Paolo Manasse, and Alessandro Prati, 2007, "Can We Predict the Next Capital Account Crisis?" *IMF Staff Papers*, Vol. 54, No. 2, pp. 270–305.

Chinn, Menzie D., and H. Ito, 2006, "What Matters for Financial Development? Capital Controls, Institutions, and Interactions," *Journal of Development Economics*, Vol. 81, No. 1, pp. 163–92.

Claessens, S., and L. Laeven, 2003, "Financial Development, Property Rights, and Growth," *Journal of Finance*, Vol. 58, No. 6, pp. 2401–36.

Clemens, Michael A., and Jeffrey G. Williamson, 2004, "Why Did the Tariff-Growth Correlation Reverse After 1950?" *Journal of Economic Growth*, Vol. 9, No. 1, pp. 5–46.

Conway, Paul, and Giuseppe Nicoletti, 2006, "Product Market Regulation in the Non-Manufacturing Sectors of OECD Countries: Measurement and Highlights," OECD Economics Department Working Paper No. 530 (Paris: Organization for Economic Cooperation and Development).

Dell'Ariccia, Giovanni, and Robert Marquez, 2006, "Lending Booms and Lending Standards," *Journal of Finance*, Vol. 61, No. 5 (October), pp. 2511–46.

Dell'Ariccia, Giovanni, and others, 2008, *Reaping the Benefits of Financial Globalization*, IMF Occasional Paper No. 264 (Washington: International Monetary Fund).

Detragiache, Enrica, Thierry Tressel, and Poonam Gupta, 2008, "Foreign Banks in Poor Countries: Theory and Evidence," *Journal of Finance*, Vol. 63, No. 5, pp. 2123–60.

di Giovanni, Julian, and Jay Shambaugh, 2008, "The Impact of Foreign Interest Rates on the Economy: The Role of the Exchange Rate Regime," *Journal of International Economics*, Vol. 74, No. 2 (March), pp. 341–61.

Dixon, William J., and Terry Boswell, 1996, "Dependency, Disarticulation and Denominator Effects: Another Look at Foreign Capital Penetration," *American Journal of Sociology*, Vol. 102, No. 2 (September), pp. 543–62.

Djankov, Simeon, Caralee McLiesh, and Andrei Shleifer, 2007, "Private Credit in 129 Countries," *Journal of Financial Economics*, Vol. 84, No. 2, pp. 299–329.

Dollar, David, and Aart Kraay, 2004, "Trade, Growth, and Poverty," *Economic Journal*, Vol. 114 (February), No. 493, pp. F22–F49.

Easterly, William, 2005, "National Policies and Economic Growth: A Reappraisal," in *Handbook of Economic Growth*, ed. by P. Aghion and S. Durlauf, Vol. 1A (Amsterdam: Elsevier).

———, and Ross Levine, 2003, "Tropics, Germs, and Crops: How Endowments Influence Economic Development," *Journal of Monetary Economics*, Vol. 50, No. 1 (January), pp. 3–47.

Edwards, Sebastian, 1993, "Trade Policy, Exchange Rates and Growth," NBER Working Paper No. 4511 (Cambridge, Massachusetts: National Bureau of Economic Research).

Edwards, Lawrence, and Robert Z. Lawrence, 2006, "South African Trade Policy Matters: Trade Performance and Trade Policy," NBER Working Paper No. 12760 (Cambridge, Massachusetts: National Bureau of Economic Research).

Fernandez, Raquel, and Dani Rodrik, 1991, "Resistance to Reform: Status Quo Bias in the Presence of Individual Specific Uncertainty," *American Economic Review*, Vol. 81, No. 55 (December), pp. 1146–55.

Fiori, Giuseppe, Giuseppe Nicoletti, Stefano Scarpetta, and Fabio Schiantarelli, 2007, "Employment Outcomes and the Interaction Between Product and Labor Market Deregulation: Are They Substitutes or Complements?" IZA Discussion Paper No. 2770 (Bonn).

Fisman, Raymond, and Inessa Love, 2004, "Financial Development and Intersectoral Allocation: A New Approach," *Journal of Finance*, Vol. 59, No. 6, pp. 2785–2807.

Frankel, Jeffrey A., and David Romer, 1999, "Does Trade Cause Growth?" *American Economic Review*, Vol. 89, No. 3 (June), pp. 379–99.

Ghosh, Atish, Charis Christofides, Jun Kim, Laura Papi, Uma Ramakrishnan, Alun Thomas, and Juan Zalduendo, 2005, "The Design of IMF-Supported Programs," IMF Occasional Paper No. 241 (Washington: International Monetary Fund).

Giavazzi, Francesco, and Guido Tabellini, 2005, "Economic and Political Liberalizations," *Journal of Monetary Economics*, Vol. 52, No. 7 (October), pp. 1297–1330.

Giuliano, Paola, Prachi Mishra, and Antonio Spilimbergo, 2008, "Democracy and Reforms," CEPR Discussion Paper No. 7194 (London: Centre for Economic Policy Research); IZA Discussion Paper No. 4032 (Bonn).

Greenwood, Jeremy, and Boyan Jovanovic, 1990, "Financial Development, Growth, and the Distribution of Income," *Journal of Political Economy*, Vol. 98, No. 5 (October), pp. 1076–1107.

Grossman, Gene M., and Elhanan Helpman, 1990, "Trade, Innovation, and Growth," *American Economic Review, Papers and Proceedings*, Vol. 80, No. 2 (May), pp. 86–91.

Haggard, Stephan, 1990, *Pathways from the Periphery: The Politics of Growth in the Newly Industrializing Countries* (Ithaca: Cornell University Press).

Hauner, David, 2009, "Public Debt and Financial Development," *Journal of Development Economics*, Vol. 88, No. 1 (January), pp. 171–83.

———, and Alessandro Prati, 2008, "Openness and Domestic Financial Liberalization: Which Comes First?" (unpublished; Washington: International Monetary Fund).

REFERENCES

Hausmann, Ricardo, Lant Pritchett, and Dani Rodrik, 2005, "Growth Accelerations," *Journal of Economic Growth*, Vol. 10, No. 4 (December), pp. 303–29.

Henry, Peter Blair, 2007, "Capital Account Liberalization: Theory, Evidence, and Speculation," *Journal of Economic Literature*, Vol. 45, No. 4 (December), pp. 887–935.

Holmstrom, Bengt, and Jean Tirole, 1997, "Financial Intermediation, Loanable Funds, and the Real Sector," *Quarterly Journal of Economics*, Vol. 112, No. 3 (August), pp. 663–91.

Høj, Jens, and others, 2006, "The Political Economy of Structural Reform: Empirical Evidence from OECD Countries," OECD Economics Department Working Paper No. 501 (Paris: Organization for Economic Cooperation and Development).

Huntington, Samuel P., 1968, *Political Order in Changing Societies* (New Haven, Connecticut: Yale University Press).

Independent Evaluation Office of the IMF (IEO), "Report on the Evaluation of the IMF's Approach to Capital Account Liberalization." Available via the Internet: www.imf.org/External/NP/ieo/2005/cal/eng/index.htm.

International Monetary Fund (IMF), 2004, *World Economic Outlook, April 2004: Advancing Structural Reforms* (Washington).

Kaminsky, Graciela, and Carmen Reinhart, 1999, "The Twin Crises: The Causes of Banking and Balance-of-Payments Problems," *American Economic Review*, Vol. 89, No. 3 (June), pp. 473–500.

Kaufmann, Daniel, Aart Kraay, and Pablo Zoido-Lobatón, 2002, "Governance Matters II—Updated Indicators for 2000/01," World Bank Policy Research Department Working Paper No. 2772 (Washington: World Bank).

Kiyotaki, Nobuhiro, and John Moore, 1997, "Credit Cycles," *Journal of Political Economy*, Vol. 105, pp. 211–48.

Kose, M. Ayhan, Eswar Prasad, Kenneth Rogoff, and Shang-Jin Wei, 2006, "Financial Globalization: A Reappraisal," NBER Working Paper No. 12484 (Cambridge, Massachusetts: National Bureau of Economic Research).

Kroszner, Randall, Luc Laeven, and Daniela Klingebiel, 2007, "Banking Crises, Financial Dependence, and Growth," *Journal of Financial Economics*, Vol. 84, No. 1, pp. 187–228.

Krueger, Anne O., 1997, "Trade Policy and Economic Development: How We Learn," *American Economic Review*, Vol. 87, No. 1 (March), pp. 1–22.

———, Maurice W. Schiff, and Alberto Valdés, eds., 1992, *The Political Economy of Agricultural Pricing Policy* (Baltimore, Maryland: Johns Hopkins University Press).

La Porta, Rafael, Florencio Lopez-de-Silanes, and Andrei Shleifer, 2002, "Government Ownership of Banks," *Journal of Finance*, Vol. 57, No. 1 (February), pp. 265–301.

La Porta, Rafael, Florencio Lopez-de-Silanes, Andrei Shleifer, and Robert Vishny, 1998, "Law and Finance," *Journal of Political Economy*, Vol. 106, No. 6 (December), pp. 1113–55.

Levine, Ross, 1997, "Financial Development and Economic Growth: Views and Agenda," *Journal of Economic Literature*, Vol. 36, No. 2 (June), pp. 668–726.

———, 2005, "Law, Endowments and Property Rights," *Journal of Economic Perspectives*, Vol. 19, No. 3 (Summer), pp. 61–88.

McGuire, Martin C., and Mancur Olson, 1996, "The Economics of Autocracy and Majority Rule: The Invisible Hand and the Use of Force," *Journal of Economic Literature*, Vol. 34, pp. 72–96.

McKinnon, Ronald I., 1973, *Money and Capital in Economic Development* (Washington: Brookings Institution).

Mishkin, Frederic, 2001, "Financial Policies and the Prevention of Financial Crises in Emerging Market Countries," NBER Working Paper No. 8087 (Cambridge, Massachusetts: National Bureau of Economic Research).

Nelson, Richard R., and Edmund S. Phelps, 1966, "Investment in Humans, Technological Diffusion, and Economic Growth," *American Economic Review*, Vol. 56, No. 1/2 (March), pp. 69–75.

Neumeyer, Pablo, and Fabrizio Perri, 2005, "Business Cycles in Emerging Economies: The Role of Interest Rates," *Journal of Monetary Economics*, Vol. 52, No. 2 (March), pp. 345–80.

Nicoletti, Giuseppe, and Stefano Scarpetta, 2003, "Regulation, Productivity and Growth: OECD Evidence," *Economic Policy*, Vol. 18, No. 36, pp. 9–72.

North, Douglass C., 1981, *Structure and Change in Economic History* (New York: W.W. Norton).

Pavcnik, Nina, 2002, "Trade Liberalization, Exit, and Productivity Improvements: Evidence from Chilean Plants," *Review of Economic Studies*, Vol. 69, No. 1 (January), pp. 245–76.

Prati, Alessandro, Martin Schindler, and Patricio Valenzuela, "Who Benefits from Capital Account Liberalization? Evidence from Firm-Level Credit Ratings Data," forthcoming IMF Working Paper (Washington: International Monetary Fund).

Pritchett, Lant, 2000, "Understanding Patterns of Economic Growth: Searching for Hills Among Plateaus, Mountains, and Plains," *World Bank Economic Review*, Vol. 14, No. 2, pp. 221–50.

Quinn, Dennis P., 1997, "The Correlates of Change in International Financial Regulation," *American Political Science Review*, Vol. 91, No. 3 (September), pp. 531–51.

———, and A. Maria Toyoda, 2008, "Does Capital Account Liberalization Lead to Economic Growth?" *Review of Financial Studies*, Vol. 21, No. 3, pp. 1403–49.

Raddatz, Claudio, 2006, "Liquidity Needs and Vulnerability to Financial Underdevelopment," *Journal of Financial Economics*, Vol. 80, No. 3, pp. 677–722.

Rajan, Raghuram, and Luigi Zingales, 1998, "Financial Dependence and Growth," *American Economic Review*, Vol. 88, No. 3, pp. 559–86.

———, 2003, "The Great Reversals: The Politics of Financial Development in the Twentieth Century," *Journal of Financial Economics*, Vol. 69, No. 1, pp. 5–50.

Ramcharan, Rodney, 2007, "Does the Exchange Rate Regime Matter for Real Shocks? Evidence from Windstorms and Earthquakes," *Journal of International Economics*, Vol. 73, No. 1, pp. 31–47.

———,"Bank Competition and the Real Cost of Interest Rate Movements," forthcoming IMF Working Paper (Washington: International Monetary Fund).

Reinhart, Carmen, and Vincent Reinhart, 2001, "What Hurts Most? G-3 Exchange Rate or Interest Rate Volatility," NBER Working Paper No. 8535 (Cambridge, Massachusetts: National Bureau of Economic Research).

References

Reinhart, Carmen, and Kenneth Rogoff, 2008, "Is the 2007 U.S. Sub-Prime Financial Crisis So Different? An International Historical Comparison," *American Economic Review*, Vol. 98, No. 2 (May), pp. 339–44.

Rodrik, Dani, 1999, "Democracies Pay Higher Wages," *Quarterly Journal of Economics*, Vol. 114, No. 3, pp. 707–38.

———, 2006, "Goodbye Washington Consensus, Hello Washington Confusion: A Review of the World Bank's Economic Growth in the 1990s: Learning from a Decade of Reform," *Journal of Economic Literature*, Vol. 44, No. 4 (December), pp. 973–87.

Roe, Mark, and Jordan Siegel, 2008, "Political Instability's Impact on Financial Development" (unpublished; Cambridge, Massachusetts: Harvard University).

Romer, Paul M., 1986, "Increasing Returns and Long-Run Growth," *Journal of Political Economy*, Vol. 94, No. 5 (October), pp. 1002–37.

Sachs, J.D., and A.M. Warner, 1995, "Economic Reform and the Process of Global Integration," *Brookings Papers on Economic Activity: 1*, pp. 1–118.

Schindler, Martin, 2009, "Measuring Financial Integration: A New Dataset," *IMF Staff Papers*, Vol. 56, No. 1, pp. 222–38.

Schumpeter, J., 1928, "The Instability of Capitalism," in *Joseph A. Schumpeter: Essays on Entrepreneurs, Innovations, Business Cycles and the Evolution of Capitalism*, ed. by R. Clemence (New Brunswick, New Jersey: Transaction Publishers, 1989).

———, 1942, *Capitalism, Socialism and Democracy* (New York: Harper and Row).

Schwarz, Gerhard, 1992, "Democracy and Market-Oriented Reform: A Love-Hate Relationship?" *Economic Education Bulletin*, Vol. 32, No. 5 (May), pp. 13–28.

Shaw, Edward S., 1973, *Financial Deepening in Economic Development* (New York: Oxford University Press).

Tressel, Thierry, 2008, "Unbundling the Effects of Reforms" (Washington: International Monetary Fund). Available via the Internet: www.imf.org/External/NP/seminars/eng/2008/strureform/index.htm.

Tressel, Thierry, and Enrica Detragiache, 2008, "Do Financial Sector Reforms Lead to Financial Development? Evidence from a New Dataset," IMF Working Paper 08/265 (Washington: International Monetary Fund).

United Nations Industrial Development Organization (UNIDO), 2006, *Annual Report*. Available via the Internet: www.unido.org/index.php?id=4800.

Vandenbussche, Jérôme, Philippe Aghion, and Costas Meghir, 2006, "Growth, Distance to Frontier and Composition of Human Capital," *Journal of Economic Growth*, Vol. 11, No. 2 (June), pp. 97–127.

van Elkan, Rachel, 1996, "Catching Up and Slowing Down: Learning and Growth Patterns in an Open Economy," *Journal of International Economics*, Vol. 41, Issues 1–2, pp. 95–111.

Wacziarg, Romain, and Karen Horn Welch, 2008, "Trade Liberalization and Growth: New Evidence," *World Bank Economic Review*, Vol. 22, No. 2, pp. 187–231.

Williamson, John, and Molly Mahar, 1998, "A Survey of Financial Liberalization," Essays in International Finance No. 211, International Finance Section, Department of Economics (Princeton, New Jersey: Princeton University).

Zalduendo, Juan, 2005, "Pace and Sequencing of Economic Policies," IMF Working Paper 05/118 (Washington: International Monetary Fund).

Recent Occasional Papers of the International Monetary Fund

268. Structural Reforms and Economic Performance in Advanced and Developing Countries, by Jonathan D. Ostry, Alessandro Prati, and Antonio Spilimbergo. 2009.
267. The Role of the Exchange Rate in Inflation-Targeting Emerging Economies, by Mark Stone, Scott Roger, Seiichi Shimizu, Anna Nordstrom, Turgut Kişinbay, and Jorge Restrepo. 2009.
266. The Debt Sustainability Framework for Low-Income Countries, by Bergljot Bjørnson Barkbu, Christian Beddies, and Marie-Hélène Le Manchec. 2008.
265. Developing Essential Financial Markets in Smaller Economies: Stylized Facts and Policy Options, by Hervé Ferhani, Mark Stone, Anna Nordstrom, and Seiichi Shimizu. 2008.
264. Reaping the Benefits of Financial Globalization, by Giovanni Dell'Ariccia, Julian di Giovanni, André Faria, Ayhan Kose, Paolo Mauro, Jonathan D. Ostry, Martin Schindler, and Marco Terrones. 2008.
263. Macroeconomic Implications of Financial Dollarization The Case of Uruguay, edited by Marco Piñón, Gaston Gelos, and Alejandro López-Mejía. 2008.
262. IMF Support and Crisis Prevention, by Atish Ghosh, Bikas Joshi, Jun Il Kim, Uma Ramakrishnan, Alun Thomas, and Juan Zalduendo. 2008.
261. Exchange Rate Assessments: CGER Methodologies, by Jaewoo Lee, Gian Maria Milesi-Ferretti, Jonathan D. Ostry, Luca Antonio Ricci, and Alessandro Prati. 2008.
260. Managing the Oil Revenue Boom: The Role of Fiscal Institutions, by Rolando Ossowski, Mauricio Villafuerte, Paulo A. Medas, and Theo Thomas. 2008.
259. Macroeconomic Consequences of Remittances, by Ralph Chami, Adolfo Barajas, Thomas Cosimano, Connel Fullenkamp, Michael Gapen, and Peter Montiel. 2008.
258. Northern Star: Canada's Path to Economic Prosperity, edited by Tamim Bayoumi, Vladimir Klyuev, and Martin Mühleisen. 2007.
257. Economic Growth and Integration in Central America, edited by Dominique Desruelle and Alfred Schipke. 2007.
256. Moving to Greater Exchange Rate Flexibility: Operational Aspects Based on Lessons from Detailed Country Experiences, by Inci Ötker-Robe and David Vávra, and a team of IMF economists. 2007.
255. Sovereign Debt Restructuring and Debt Sustainability: An Analysis of Recent Cross-Country Experience, by Harald Finger and Mauro Mecagni. 2007.
254. Country Insurance: The Role of Domestic Policies, by Törbjörn Becker, Olivier Jeanne, Paolo Mauro, Jonathan D. Ostry, and Romain Rancière. 2007.
253. The Macroeconomics of Scaling Up Aid: Lessons from Recent Experience, by Andrew Berg, Shekhar Aiyar, Mumtaz Hussain, Shaun Roache, Tokhir Mirzoev, and Amber Mahone. 2007.
252. Growth in the Central and Eastern European Countries of the European Union, by Susan Schadler, Ashoka Mody, Abdul Abiad, and Daniel Leigh. 2006.
251. The Design and Implementation of Deposit Insurance Systems, by David S. Hoelscher, Michael Taylor, and Ulrich H. Klueh. 2006.
250. Designing Monetary and Fiscal Policy in Low-Income Countries, by Abebe Aemro Selassie, Benedict Clements, Shamsuddin Tareq, Jan Kees Martijn, and Gabriel Di Bella. 2006.
249. Official Foreign Exchange Intervention, by Shogo Ishi, Jorge Iván Canales-Kriljenko, Roberto Guimarães, and Cem Karacadag. 2006.
248. Labor Market Performance in Transition: The Experience of Central and Eastern European Countries, by Jerald Schiff, Philippe Egoumé-Bossogo, Miho Ihara, Tetsuya Konuki, and Kornélia Krajnyák. 2006.
247. Rebuilding Fiscal Institutions in Post-Conflict Countries, by Sanjeev Gupta, Shamsuddin Tareq, Benedict Clements, Alex Segura-Ubiergo, Rina Bhattacharya, and Todd Mattina. 2005.
246. Experience with Large Fiscal Adjustments, by George C. Tsibouris, Mark A. Horton, Mark J. Flanagan, and Wojciech S. Maliszewski. 2005.
245. Budget System Reform in Emerging Economies: The Challenges and the Reform Agenda, by Jack Diamond. 2005.
244. Monetary Policy Implementation at Different Stages of Market Development, by a staff team led by Bernard J. Laurens. 2005.

243. Central America: Global Integration and Regional Cooperation, edited by Markus Rodlauer and Alfred Schipke. 2005.
242. Turkey at the Crossroads: From Crisis Resolution to EU Accession, by a staff team led by Reza Moghadam. 2005.
241. The Design of IMF-Supported Programs, by Atish Ghosh, Charis Christofides, Jun Kim, Laura Papi, Uma Ramakrishnan, Alun Thomas, and Juan Zalduendo. 2005.
240. Debt-Related Vulnerabilities and Financial Crises: An Application of the Balance Sheet Approach to Emerging Market Countries, by Christoph Rosenberg, Ioannis Halikias, Brett House, Christian Keller, Jens Nystedt, Alexander Pitt, and Brad Setser. 2005.
239. GEM: A New International Macroeconomic Model, by Tamim Bayoumi, with assistance from Douglas Laxton, Hamid Faruqee, Benjamin Hunt, Philippe Karam, Jaewoo Lee, Alessandro Rebucci, and Ivan Tchakarov. 2004.
238. Stabilization and Reforms in Latin America: A Macroeconomic Perspective on the Experience Since the Early 1990s, by Anoop Singh, Agnès Belaisch, Charles Collyns, Paula De Masi, Reva Krieger, Guy Meredith, and Robert Rennhack. 2005.
237. Sovereign Debt Structure for Crisis Prevention, by Eduardo Borensztein, Marcos Chamon, Olivier Jeanne, Paolo Mauro, and Jeromin Zettelmeyer. 2004.
236. Lessons from the Crisis in Argentina, by Christina Daseking, Atish R. Ghosh, Alun Thomas, and Timothy Lane. 2004.
235. A New Look at Exchange Rate Volatility and Trade Flows, by Peter B. Clark, Natalia Tamirisa, and Shang-Jin Wei, with Azim Sadikov and Li Zeng. 2004.
234. Adopting the Euro in Central Europe: Challenges of the Next Step in European Integration, by Susan M. Schadler, Paulo F. Drummond, Louis Kuijs, Zuzana Murgasova, and Rachel N. van Elkan. 2004.
233. Germany's Three-Pillar Banking System: Cross-Country Perspectives in Europe, by Allan Brunner, Jörg Decressin, Daniel Hardy, and Beata Kudela. 2004.
232. China's Growth and Integration into the World Economy: Prospects and Challenges, edited by Eswar Prasad. 2004.
231. Chile: Policies and Institutions Underpinning Stability and Growth, by Eliot Kalter, Steven Phillips, Marco A. Espinosa-Vega, Rodolfo Luzio, Mauricio Villafuerte, and Manmohan Singh. 2004.
230. Financial Stability in Dollarized Countries, by Anne-Marie Gulde, David Hoelscher, Alain Ize, David Marston, and Gianni De Nicolò. 2004.
229. Evolution and Performance of Exchange Rate Regimes, by Kenneth S. Rogoff, Aasim M. Husain, Ashoka Mody, Robin Brooks, and Nienke Oomes. 2004.
228. Capital Markets and Financial Intermediation in The Baltics, by Alfred Schipke, Christian Beddies, Susan M. George, and Niamh Sheridan. 2004.
227. U.S. Fiscal Policies and Priorities for Long-Run Sustainability, edited by Martin Mühleisen and Christopher Towe. 2004.
226. Hong Kong SAR: Meeting the Challenges of Integration with the Mainland, edited by Eswar Prasad, with contributions from Jorge Chan-Lau, Dora Iakova, William Lee, Hong Liang, Ida Liu, Papa N'Diaye, and Tao Wang. 2004.
225. Rules-Based Fiscal Policy in France, Germany, Italy, and Spain, by Teresa Dában, Enrica Detragiache, Gabriel di Bella, Gian Maria Milesi-Ferretti, and Steven Symansky. 2003.
224. Managing Systemic Banking Crises, by a staff team led by David S. Hoelscher and Marc Quintyn. 2003.
223. Monetary Union Among Member Countries of the Gulf Cooperation Council, by a staff team led by Ugo Fasano. 2003.
222. Informal Funds Transfer Systems: An Analysis of the Informal Hawala System, by Mohammed El Qorchi, Samuel Munzele Maimbo, and John F. Wilson. 2003.
221. Deflation: Determinants, Risks, and Policy Options, by Manmohan S. Kumar. 2003.

Note: For information on the titles and availability of Occasional Papers not listed, please consult the IMF's *Publications Catalog* or contact IMF Publication Services.